GLOBE

Trave

TANZANIA

Graham Mercer

NEW
HOLLAND

NEW
HOLLAND

```
★★★ Highly recommended
 ★★ Recommended
  ★ See if you can
```

Sixth edition published in 2013
by New Holland Publishers (UK) Ltd
London • Cape Town • Sydney • Auckland
10 9 8 7 6 5 4 3 2 1
website: www.newhollandpublishers.com

Garfield House, 86 Edgware Road
London W2 2EA, United Kingdom

Wembley Square, First Floor, Solan Road
Gardens, Cape Town 8001, South Africa

Unit 1, 66 Gibbes Street
Chatswood, NSW 2067, Australia

218 Lake Road, Northcote,
Auckland, New Zealand

Distributed in the USA by
The Globe Pequot Press, Connecticut

ISBN 978 1 78009 391 8

This guidebook has been written by independent
authors and updaters. The information therein represents their impartial opinion, and neither they nor the
publishers accept payment in return for including in
the book or writing more favourable reviews of any
of the establishments. Whilst every effort has been
made to ensure that this guidebook is as accurate
and up to date as possible, please be aware that the
facts quoted are subject to change, particularly the
price of food, transport and accommodation. The
Publisher accepts no responsibility or liability for any
loss, injury or inconvenience incurred by readers or
travellers using this guide.

Keep us Current
Information in travel guides is apt to change, which
is why we regularly update our guides. We'd be
grateful to receive feedback if you've noted something we should include in our updates. If you
have new information, please share it with us by
writing to the Publishing Manager, Globetrotter, at
the office nearest to you (addresses on this page).
The most significant contribution to each new edition will receive a free copy of the updated guide.

Publishing Manager: Thea Grobbelaar
DTP Cartographic Manager: Genené Hart
Editors: Thea Grobbelaar, Carla Redelinghuys,
Nicky Steenkamp, Melany Porter, Donald Reid
Design and DTP: Nicole Bannister, Lellyn
Creamer, Sonya Cupido
Cartographers: Tracey-Lee Fredericks, Luyolo
Ndlotyeni, Marisa Roman, William Smuts

Reproduction by Hirt & Carter (Pty) Ltd, Cape Town
Printed and bound by Craft Print International Ltd,
Singapore

Dedication:
To my father, who gave me my love of wildlife
and travel, and to my mother, who believed in me.

Photographic Credits:
Peter Blackwell/IOA, all photographs except the
following: **Nick Ledger/awl-images.com**, cover;
Nigel J. Dennis/DD Photography, page 103;
Martin Edge, pages 49–54; **Corrie Hansen**, page
118; **Graham Mercer**, pages 24, 32, 33; **Peter
Ribton/IOA**, pages 19, 28, 31, 35, 36, 37, 38, 44,
67. [IOA = Images of Africa.]

Acknowledgements:
I would like to thank Mohamed Amin, Ms Patricia
Barrett, Ms Jamila Sumra, Ms Louise Whittle,
Gemini, of Emslies Travels, all the lovely people at
New Holland Publishing, the International School
of Tanganyika, my long-suffering safari partners
(Kevin Bartlett, Hamid Bharmal, John Boyce, Arshad
Hussain, Barry Whitemore and my wife Anjum) and
all the various rangers and game scouts of the
Tanzanian National Parks and Game Reserves.

Front Cover: *A man and his boat, Jambiani.*
Title Page: *Fishing boat on Zanzibar's east coast.*

CONTENTS

1. Introducing Tanzania

Tanzania, despite a wealth of natural resources, is among the world's poorest countries, and at times among its most exasperating. For visitors it can often be expensive, hot and unsophisticated. But few countries in the world offer so many natural attractions and so much adventure.

Its scenery alone, from the high snows of **Kilimanjaro** to the coral sands of **Zanzibar**, is splendid. And yet these landscapes are little more than stages for a whole cast of wildlife spectaculars, including the greatest of natural double-acts, **Ngorongoro** and the **Serengeti**, scene of the annual migration which involves more than two million animals.

Also in the north is Lake **Manyara**, famous for flamingoes and tree-climbing lions, and **Tarangire**, whilst in the south lie the no less exciting wildernesses of **Ruaha** and the **Selous**. Westwards, bordering **Lake Tanganyika**, rise the mountains of **Mahale** and **Gombe** chimpanzee havens, with the remote, landlocked and little-visited sanctuary of **Katavi** nearby.

Tanzania's people, generally friendly and welcoming without being servile, range from Maasai pastoralists armed with spears to cosmopolitan city dwellers. Their history begins with man's first footsteps, printed in volcanic ash millions of years ago, and extends to the present day through the remarkable Swahili civilization, the slave trade, the Zanzibari sultanate and the great age of exploration, when men such as Livingstone and Stanley strode the land.

For those who can rise above its various challenges, Tanzania, the 'real Africa', awaits with an outstretched hand and a ready *Karibuni!* – 'Welcome!'

TOP ATTRACTIONS

*** **Serengeti National Park:** spectacular animal migration.
*** **Ngorongoro Crater:** Noah's Ark shipwrecked in a volcanic bowl.
*** **Selous Game Reserve:** huge wilderness.
*** **Ruaha National Park:** another wonderful wilderness.
*** **Mount Kilimanjaro:** highest mountain in Africa.
*** **Zanzibar:** history, diving, fine beaches.
** **Tarangire National Park:** huge elephant herds, abundant wildlife in the dry season.
** **Lake Manyara:** elephants, birds, striking scenery.

◀ *Opposite: The active volcano and Maasai 'Mountain of God' (Ol Doinyo Lengai) in the Rift Valley.*

- Visible from space, stretching from Jordan to the Zambezi, and more than 9700km (6000 miles) long, the Rift is Tanzania's main geographical feature.
- It has been formed by the intense underground stresses caused by shifts in the Earth's tectonic plates over a period of 20 million years. Even today there is turbulence below ground.
- For much of its length the valley is characterized by steep, sharply defined walls on both its eastern and western sides.
- Between the Danakil Depression in northern Ethiopia and Lake Tanganyika there are at least 30 active or semi-active volcanoes.

THE LAND

Tanzania measures 945,087 km^2 (364,898 sq miles) in area and contains the highest mountain in Africa, Kilimanjaro (5896m; 19,340ft), and part of its deepest lake, Tanganyika (358m; 1174ft). But statistics alone can convey nothing of the variety or attractiveness of Tanzania's topography, which ranges from mighty volcanic and ancient crystalline mountains to rolling table-land, from great lakes to seemingly endless grasslands, dense miombo woodland to palm-fringed coral sands.

The land is riven north to south by the eastern arm of the **Great Rift Valley**, the western fork of which, in the shape of Lake Tanganyika, helps to form Tanzania's western border. The country's eastern border is deter-mined by the Indian Ocean, and in the south by the Ruvuma River. To the north the border with Kenya is more political than natural, except for a distinct kink around Kilimanjaro.

Mountains and Valleys

The best-known mountain in all Africa is surely **Kilimanjaro**, affectionately known as 'Kili'. Its familiar snow-capped dome rises regally from the Maasai plains in the north of the country. Close by is **Meru**, another beautiful volcanic mountain, and further west other orphans of violence proliferate in and around the Rift. Among them is Ol Doinyo Lengai, 'the Mountain of God' to the Maasai, and still active.

▼ Below: The dazzling snows of Kilimanjaro, only 3° south of the equator.

Around Lengai the Rift is dramatic, with abrupt walls to east and west rising to between 270 and 680m (800 to 2000ft) above the floor. The sector of the Tanzanian Rift which most tourists cross, between Makuyuni and Lake Manyara, is less impressive as the eastern wall has eroded, though there are excellent views from the heights of the western escarpment. Beyond the Rift rise the **Crater Highlands**, including Ngorongoro, the most famous crater (more properly caldera) on Earth, and home to as many as 20,000 big game animals.

South of Kilimanjaro, the broken ranges of the **Eastern Arc** mountains ride south in craggy splendour. The light and cloud effects along these mountains, the **Pare** and the **Usambara**, can be spectacular. Further south the ranges swing inland to become the **Uluguru**s and **Udzungwa**s, before merging into the **Southern Highlands**, a beautiful region centred around the small towns of Iringa and Mbeya. Southeast of Mbeya the **Livingstone Mountains**, named after the celebrated explorer, shelve with precipitous grandeur into the waters of Lake Malawi (still known as Lake Nyasa in Tanzania and currently much disputed).

▲ *Above: A typical first view of Ngorongoro, from the southern rim of the crater.*

TOURING TANZANIA

Tanzania is a very poor country with a gradually developing tourism sector. Things are improving, but sometimes simple things can take much longer than anticipated, so bear in mind that a tour including Serengeti, Ngorongoro, Kilimanjaro and Zanzibar, for example, will easily fill a fortnight.

Visitors are advised to employ the services of a reputable tour company, arranged before or after arrival in Tanzania. For information on reputable tour companies and what they offer, *see* the Travel Tips section at the back of the book.

▲ *Above: The Rufiji River, life-blood of the mighty Selous Game Reserve.*

MONSTERS OF THE DEEP

Tanzania's inland waters can be huge and violent, as can some of the monsters living in them. Lake Victoria is the size of Scotland and Lake Tanganyika, almost deep enough to engulf five Eiffel Towers standing one on top of each other, is longer than Portugal. Both lakes are subject to fierce and sudden storms with 6m (20ft) swells, but beneath their surface live creatures equally daunting. The Nile Perch can exceed 227kg (500lb) and has been known to attack boats. A lungfish in Lake Victoria grows as long as 2m (7ft) and is capable of removing human fingers. Not surprisingly, stories of African equivalents to the Loch Ness monster are traded in the lakeside fishing communities.

The mountains and the Rift dominate their immediate landscapes, but the characteristic topography of Tanzania is the undulating **central plateau**, which averages 1200m (4000ft) above sea level. This tableland, extending through much of the country, can be divided (roughly from northwest to southeast) according to its vegetation. In the northeast open grasslands and Acacia-Commiphora woodland predominates, while in the south miombo woodland (mainly Brachystegia and Julbernadia) covers much of the landscape. The plateau, unvisited by most tourists, can be a place of great beauty, especially in the rains.

Inland Waters

Tanzania contains more surface water than any other African country. It is drained by a network of rivers, many of them seasonal, and along its western border lie the great lakes of **Victoria**, **Tanganyika** and **Malawi**. Victoria is the second largest and Tanganyika the second deepest lake in the world. The largest river is the **Rufiji**, which drains a vast 177,400km^2 (68,500 sq miles) of land. Other significant rivers are the **Pangani**, which flows south from Kilimanjaro, the **Wami**, which waters two game areas, Mikumi and Saadani, and the **Ruvuma**, which forms Tanzania's southern border with Mozambique. All empty into the Indian Ocean.

Seas and Shores

Tanzania's 800km (500-mile) coastline is typically tropical, with a coral reef and long stretches of near-white sand, often backed by groves of coconut palm or stands of feathery casuarina. Here and there this congruity of sea and sand is broken by estuaries or mangrove swamps, and in places low limestone cliffs and sea caves.

Fascinating ruins at **Kilwa**, **Bagamoyo** and in **Zanzibar** tell of the coast's history. **Bagamoyo**, just north of Dar es Salaam, was the mainland terminus of both the slave and ivory trade and the exploration of the interior in the 19th century. Once capital of German East Africa, it lost its status when the Germans moved to Dar es Salaam in 1891. North of Bagamoyo is another interesting stretch of coast, including Saadani National Park, Pangani and Tanga.

Zanzibar lies low on the horizon opposite Bagamoyo, and often in cloud, as if mindful of its somewhat murky past. Nowadays, however, both Zanzibar and **Pemba** (to the north) are engaged in more innocent business, bringing in boatloads of tourists rather than slaves. A similar emphasis also inspires **Mafia Island**, which is further south and known for its big game fishing, snorkelling and diving. A marine park is now established there.

MORE MONSTERS OF THE DEEP

Tanzania's offshore waters offer superb fishing. Kingfish, barracuda, giant trevally and grouper are to be found year round. From December to March and in August and September sailfish, wahoo and dorado provide exciting sport, with yellow fin tuna from August to December. And if fishing doesn't appeal, you might bump into humpback whales (hopefully not literally). The whales migrate north in July and August to the east of Zanzibar and Pemba. Around October they return, passing between the islands and the shore. Sperm whales and great white sharks are also found in Tanzanian waters.

▼ Below: Secluded sands and exposed coral at Matemwe, on Zanzibar's northeast coast.

INTRODUCING TANZANIA

SHORT RAINS, LONG RAINS

On the equator, the sun passes its zenith twice a year. Because of the phenomenon known as the intertropical convergence zone, about four weeks later the northeast and southwest trade winds converge, causing torrential rainfall typical of the tropics. Generally speaking, the **Short Rains** (mid-October to mid-December) are lighter and much less predictable than the **Long Rains** (mid-March to mid-May). Even during the long rains there can be dry and sunny days in most areas, though visitors can assume that April, throughout East Africa, will be pretty wet. This is not necessarily a deterrent to travel. Most parks and tourist attractions are quite accessible even in April, and in terms of scenery often at their best.

▶ *Opposite: Flat-topped acacia give attractive definition to the grasslands of Serengeti National Park.*

Climate

The climate of much of Tanzania is dictated by the two seasonal Indian Ocean trade winds, or monsoons, though across the country there are many local variations, mainly due to altitude differences and by the presence, in the west, of large bodies of surface water.

The northeast trades (*kasikazi* in Kiswahili) blow from late December to the beginning of March, bringing the **Short Rains**, the less welcome heat of the Arabian Gulf, and a sometimes oppressive sultriness to the coastal regions. On its tail, from approximately mid-March to mid-May, come the **Long Rains**, *mwaka*. The southeast trades (*kusi*), which generally blow from May to the end of September, curve in from the southern oceans, bringing pleasantly cooler, less humid air across the coast and far inland. Their arrival marks the beginning of the five- or six-month **dry season**, when plant growth, especially away from the coast, comes to a standstill and many watercourses cease to flow.

Because of the country's varied topography, the climate of Tanzania is not as predictable as tropical climates often are. Rain might fall, or fail to fall, when least expected, and the two distinct rainy seasons, characteristic of equatorial regions, will sometimes merge into one or vary considerably in length and intensity. On the whole, however, visitors to northern Tanzania can expect to find dry weather between June and the end of October, and a shorter dry spell from early January to mid-March. Further south the two rainy spells might not be so distinct, with variable precipitation likely from mid-November through to about mid-March.

Temperatures are also changeable, ranging from an average day-time figure of 30°C (86°F) at the coast, where the humidity is often high, to Arctic temperatures at the sum-

COMPARATIVE CLIMATE CHART	NGORONGORO				ZANZIBAR				IRINGA			
	SUM	AUT	WIN	SPR	SUM	AUT	WIN	SPR	SUM	AUT	WIN	SPR
	JAN	APR	JULY	OCT	JAN	APR	JULY	OCT	JAN	APR	JULY	OCT
AVE TEMP. °F	70	66	64	70	81	79	66	79	70	68	66	72
AVE TEMP. °C	21	19	18	21	27	26	19	26	21	20	19	22
SEA TEMP. °F	n/a	n/a	n/a	n/a	79	84	81	77	n/a	n/a	n/a	n/a
SEA TEMP. °C	n/a	n/a	n/a	n/a	26	29	27	25	n/a	n/a	n/a	n/a
DAYS OF RAINFALL	10	13	2	8	8	12	6	11	13	4	0	5
RAINFALL mm	99	114	9	74	94	232	46	155	128	25	1	63

mit of Kilimanjaro. They vary seasonally as well, and visitors can generally expect cooler weather from mid-May to mid-November, particularly between early evening and mid-morning, though the sun can still be searingly hot at the height of the day. But even at the hottest times, cooling breezes or showers of rain can help to make life more tolerable.

Plant Life

In keeping with the variations in Tanzania's topography and climate, the country's plant life is richly diverse in form and distribution. Along the coast, **coconuts**, **casuarinas** and **mangroves** are common. Small (and sadly diminishing) remnants of coastal forest occur in patches a little way inland from the shoreline.

Further inland the natural tree cover in the south-western half of the country is **miombo**, which gives way in the north to the open parkland of flat-topped **acacia** and 'apple orchard' **commiphora**, which so many people associate with East Africa. Undulating grasslands make up large areas of the Serengeti, the Rift Valley and the plains below Kilimanjaro and Meru. These and other mountains are partly clothed in **montane forest**, and Kilimanjaro's altitude produces bands of fascinating and sometimes indigenous species of flora, including the **giant heathers** along the upper fringes of the rainforest, and the **giant lobelias** and **groundsels** of the alpine moorland zone.

Elsewhere in the country, where conditions are suitable, the **baobab** grows in corpulent and sometimes archaic grandeur, in places forming magnificent forests. And along the watercourses **figs**, **tamarinds** and **palms** add a welcome touch of green to the dessicated bush, even at the height of the dry season.

Wild flowers do not always grow in great profusion, but there is a wealth of species, and when the rains come the bush can hum with vitality and colour. Some species are unique,

EXOTIC BLOSSOMS

The trees and shrubs in Tanzania's towns are as cosmopolitan as the human population. Commonly seen species include:
- Jacaranda, Pride of Bolivia, and bouganvillea, all from South America.
- Flamboyant, the 'Zanzibar Christmas Tree', from Madagascar.
- Various species of hibiscus, originally from China.
- Pride of Barbados, and Indian almond, which speak for themselves.
- Bottlebrush and Australian flame, both from Australasia. These 'expats' look beautiful and provide welcome shade, but they would struggle to survive alongside the thorny acacias and sinewy figs out in the 'real' world of the bush.

▶ *Opposite: Lady killers – Serengeti National Park.*

such as the endangered African violets, and Kilimanjaro's *Impatiens kilimanjari*, an endemic red and yellow varietal of 'busy Lizzie'.

Cultivated plants include coffee, tea, cashew nuts, cloves, sugar and sisal, all important to Tanzania's economy. Maize, wheat, millet, sorghum, cassava, and rice are grown for home consumption, together with bananas and mangoes. A wide variety of vegetables and fruits come from the fertile central and northern regions of Kilimanjaro, Lushoto, Morogoro and Iringa.

Wildlife

There are many reasons for coming to Tanzania, but the main attraction is undoubtedly the country's wildlife and the magnificent habitats in which it is found. An astonishing 25% of Tanzania's land area is given over to protected wildlife zones, and 20% of Africa's larger mammals are to be found within the country. A dozen or more of these, often including **lion**, **elephant**, **buffalo**, **hippo**, **giraffe** and several **antelope** or **gazelle** can easily be seen in the briefest trip to most national parks. Safari guides, on popular tours to the northern parks, feel disappointed if they haven't shown their clients at least 30 species of larger mammals, from the **Big Five** down to hyrax and mongooses. The Big Five as the old hunters knew them – lion, leopard, elephant, buffalo and rhino – are found (with the sad exception of rhino) in most of Tanzania's parks and reserves, though leopards can be elusive. **Cheetah** can usually be seen in the Serengeti (they occur elsewhere but not in such numbers) and rhino in Ngorongoro Crater. There are also **reptiles** such as crocodiles, monitor lizards and snakes, although snakes are seldom seen. Keen birders, assuming they visit several parks and are accompanied by a knowledgeable guide, can expect to tick off well over 100 species (more than 1100 bird species are listed for Tanzania).

It should not be forgotten that Tanzania has Serengetis of the sea as well as the land. The Indian Ocean is rich in fascinating marine mammals, fish and reptiles, and Lake Tanganyika is full of endemic creatures. The rare and endangered **dugong**, several **turtles** and a whole host of **whales**, **dolphins**, **sharks** and **tropical fish** are found around and beyond the coral gardens of the coastal reefs. Marine parks are now being set up.

Conservation in Tanzania

Until recently Tanzania's attitude towards conservation was widely admired, but President Kikwete's government has changed all that. Its determination to build a commercial highway across the Serengeti has shocked and angered wildlife enthusiasts around the world, while plans to extract soda ash from Lake Natron, the premier breeding ground for the iconic Lesser Flamingo, has aroused condemnation among bird lovers. Meanwhile uranium is being mined and a huge dam scheduled to be built in the Selous Game Reserve (a World Heritage site), while Kikwete is rumoured to be planning to nullify an application to grant similar World Heritage status to the unique, endemics-rich Udzungwa and Uluguru mountains.

Organized poaching, apparently orchestrated by at least one high-powered syndicate, is again devastating elephant populations and threatening Tanzania's few remaining rhinos. Poaching for 'bush meat' is also increasing – outside the sanctuaries, lions, victims of habitat loss, have declined dramatically as their prey species diminish and they turn to stock-raiding.

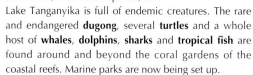

THE MAGNIFICENT SEVEN

Where you can spot them:
● **Lion:** widespread, though decreasing rapidly outside protected areas. *Almost guaranteed* in Serengeti and Ngorongoro, and usually seen in Tarangire, Manyara, Mikumi, Ruaha, Selous and Katavi.
● **Leopard:** widespread but best chances are along Seronera Valley, Serengeti, Tarangire and Ruaha.
● **Cheetah:** often seen in the southern Serengeti, on the plains around Ngorongoro, and less often in Tarangire, Ruaha, and Selous.
● **Wild Dog:** much endangered, with unpredictable movements. Likeliest places are Selous and Ruaha.
● **Rhino:** Ngorongoro crater.
● **Elephant:** Serengeti, Ngorongoro, Manyara, Tarangire, Mikumi, Ruaha, Selous and Katavi.
● **Chimpanzee:** Gombe Stream, Mahale Mountains.

▲ *Above: Game drive through the Selous Game Reserve.*

Vultures are also diminishing, partly because the poisoned baits often used to kill lions also kill them and other scavengers.

As elsewhere, the supreme threat comes from unplanned increases in human populations. Consequences in Tanzania, apart from habitat loss, include water and air pollution, widespread deforestation, the conversion of bush into charcoal for domestic use, the degradation of mangrove swamps, and the destruction of coral reefs by dynamite fishing.

In a country where police, national park rangers and game scouts are poorly paid and motivated, and where corruption is often a way of life, the fight to conserve the country's natural assets is always going to be difficult. But it must be remembered that many officials in and outside the national parks and reserves do a demanding job with honesty and integrity for little material reward, despite the shabby examples set by certain colleagues, politicians and opportunistic, self-interested outsiders.

On the credit side, new parks (such as Mkomazi) have been gazetted and established ones expanded. Elephant populations in most parks seem to be stable or increasing, and black rhino are being bred and gradually released in certain areas. In Dar es Salaam, with President Kikwete's blessing, a project is now being launched to rid the city of its Indian House Crows, introduced in the 1890s. If successful, the traumatic impact of the crows upon local bird life will be much reduced, allowing many indigenous species to re-establish themselves. A great deal of other good work, in terms of research or the attempted resolution of conservational issues, is going on elsewhere, involving expatriates as well as Tanzanians.

GOING UP IN SMOKE

One of the biggest conservation problems in Tanzania is deforestation, and one of its biggest causes is charcoal burning. Sacks of charcoal can often be seen along roadsides awaiting buyers. Most of it goes to Dar es Salaam or other urban areas, where consumption is high. It is the cheapest form of energy for cooking. The charcoal burners of the bush belong to an ancient line of craftsmen, but their fascinating skills were once practiced in less populous times, causing little lasting destruction. But it takes 10 tonnes of raw wood to produce one tonne of charcoal, and today Tanzania's woodland is disappearing at a rate of up to 400,000ha (1500 sq miles) a year.

HISTORY IN BRIEF

East Africa has been called the 'Cradle of Mankind', though this distinction must presently rest with Ethiopia, where hominid remains dating back 4.4 million years have recently been discovered. Nevertheless, Tanzania's Olduvai Gorge, in the Ngorongoro Conservation Unit, has provided us with Nutcracker Man (*Australopithacus boisei*) and Handy Man (*Homo habilis*), both about 1.8 million years old, and, at the time of their discovery, significant landmarks in the study of man's past. In 1978 at Laetoli, just south of Olduvai, Mary Leakey found footprints of three upright-standing hominids in compacted volcanic ash, which had powdered the plains 3.7 million years ago.

More recently the aboriginal inhabitants of present-day Tanzania were hunter-gatherers. Other tribes gradually moved in, seeking better land and displacing or absorbing the aborigines. The newcomers were Bantu, entering from the regions between the western lakes. By AD 1300 they had spread into the areas of heavy rainfall, leaving the plains to the Nilo-Hamitic pastoralists who came down later from the north.

Arrival of the Arabs

The first non-Africans to visit the area were probably **traders** from Arabia, Persia and India, who eventually settled along the coast with the aim of taking better advantage of trading opportunities or simply because the fertile, relatively peaceful coastal strip was preferable to conditions at home. Being dependent upon the monsoons they would have been obliged, in any case, to stay in East Africa for months at a time.

This settlement of the 'Land of Zinj' (Land of Blacks) began with **Arab** immigrants in about AD 800, who were joined 400 years later by **Shirazis** (originally from Persia). Inter-marriage between these newcomers

DHOWS

As late as 1946, 678 foreign dhows came into Zanzibar, a total probably unsurpassed in East African history. But the large and beautiful *baghlahs* and *booms* (the word 'dhow' is generic and there are many specific types) have become extinct, or are almost so. *Jahazis* of over 9m (30ft) can still be seen, along with smaller *daus* and *mashuas*, the outrigger *ngalawas* and the dug-out *mtumbwis*. Dhows ply the Zanzibar Channel, carrying anything from cloves or cement to chicken feed or corrugated iron, yet few craft evoke the romance of the eastern seas more strongly, leaning into a marbled blue sea, their lateen sails stretched into graceful curves by a steady monsoon.

▼ *Below: All our yesterdays; relics of early man in Olduvai Gorge Museum.*

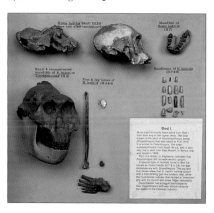

▲ *Above: A Swahili girl stands by an ornate Zanzibar door.*
▶ *Opposite: Caves used to hide slaves after the trade was abolished in 1873 at Mangapwani on Zanzibar.*

and local Africans produced the **Swahili** people who soon established a rich and enterprising civilization. The resulting language, Swahili, is now spoken throughout East Africa.

Arab and African lifestyles effectively fused into the common Swahili culture, and by the 15th century 37 Swahili towns existed in Zinj. Despite constant bickering among these tiny 'city-states', commerce flourished until 1498, when the arrival of Portuguese navigator **Vasco da Gama**, stopping off from his remarkable passage to India, signalled a new era.

The Portuguese Centuries

Da Gama, and the compatriots who followed in his wake two years later, were not interested in colonizing Zinj, and made little effort to explore the interior. The Portuguese who found themselves on the Swahili coast were guardians rather than settlers, maintaining bases from which ships could be provisioned and the safety of the shipping lanes between Portuguese territories in

HISTORICAL CALENDAR

3.7 million years BC hominids leave footprints at Laetoli.
750,000 years BC Volcanic Kilimanjaro formed.
AD800 Arab traders settle on East African coast.
AD1000 Bantu tribes moving in from west; on coast Swahili civilization beginning.
1498 Arrival of Vasco da Gama. Portuguese rule coast.
1600 British ships appearing in Indian Ocean.
1699 Omani Arabs seize East coast. Portuguese retreat.
1800 Maasai spreading southwards into northern Tanzania.
1832 Seyyid Said transfers seat of sultanate from Oman to Zanzibar. Era of prosperity for Zanzibar begins.

1860 John Speke leaves Zanzibar to find source of the Nile.
1871 Stanley sets out from Zanzibar to find Livingstone.
1873 Livingstone dies. Zanzibar slave market closes.
1890 Anglo-German agreement. Mainland Tanzania becomes German East Africa, Zanzibar a British protectorate.
1914–18 World War I. After fierce campaign in East Africa Britain takes control of what becomes known as Tanganyika.
1961 Tanganyika gains independence; Zanzibar follows in 1963.
1964 Revolution in Zanzibar. Sultan flees. Three months later Zanzibar and

mainland become United Republic of Tanzania.
1978 Idi Amin's Ugandan army invades western Tanzania. Repelled and defeated.
1985 President Nyerere is succeeded by Ali Hassan Mwinyi.
1995 First multi-party elections; Benjamin Mkapa is elected president. (Re-elected in 2000.)
1999 Julius Nyerere dies.
2005 Jakaya Kikwete elected President.
2010 Kikwete elected for a second five-year term. In Zanzibar a government of national unity is established, headed by a new President, Ali Mohamed Shein.

Muscat, Goa and Mozambique secured. They were, however, well armed and ruthless. By 1509 the Swahili towns, already disunited, were subdued, with Kilwa sacked and Mombasa reduced to rubble. For the next two centuries the Portuguese occupied the coast, but they were always insecure, threatened by Turkish pirates and later, at the beginning of the 17th century, by the appearance of an increasing number of British ships.

By 1729, with their Indian empire in disarray, the Portuguese were forced to flee by the **Omani Arabs**. The Omanis had raided Mombasa in 1660, and after the stronghold at Fort Jesus fell, the Portuguese sailed south to Mozambique, leaving little behind but bad feeling, rusting cannon, and a host of introduced crops, such as cassava, pineapples, pawpaws and groundnuts.

The Rule of Zanzibar

The Omani sultan, distracted by feuding and rivalries at home, had to leave his newly won East African possessions to various representatives. The Mazrui family, which had been given authority for Mombasa, took advantage of a change of leadership in Oman and declared an independent sheikdom, attacking other settlements. In response to pleas for help, the new sultan in Oman, **Seyyid Said**, sailed south, capturing Pemba in 1822. He was thwarted in his attempts to win back Mombasa, but he fell in love with Zanzibar, and in 1832 transferred the seat of his Imamate to the island. Said was the power behind Zanzibar's rise, establishing the clove industry that was to prove so profitable, and he was to hold considerable influence over events both along the coastal strip and deep into the interior. He also boosted the turnover of that more sordid business, the trade in human lives.

Slaving had gone on for at least 2000 years, but under the Zanzibar sultans it reached its awful peak. Up to 30,000 slaves a year were brought to Zanzibar in the early 1870s, to work the clove plantations or to be sold in the market. Great caravans left Bagamoyo for the interior, returning with slaves and ivory. Zanzibari traders made fortunes, and helped to depopulate huge areas.

A MOVEABLE FEAST

The Moroccan traveller, **Ibn Batuta**, visited the East African coast in 1331, and remarked that the people he found were 'very fat and corpulent'. Though the Swahilis enjoyed a rich diet, they couldn't compete in terms of protein sufficiency with the Zimba, another coastal people – with a taste for human flesh. When the Portuguese attacked the city states in Zinj, they enlisted the help of these cannibals, who literally ate their way from Kilwa to Malindi. They devoured dogs, lizards and rats, as well as the citizens of Kilwa and Mombasa. At Malindi the Portuguese, perhaps afraid of appearing on their menu, turned on the Zimba, almost wiping them out.

SULTAN SAID

Sultan Said, aged 15, succeeded to the Omani throne by murdering his cousin, and his first sight of East Africa was at the head of an invading army. Yet Said was more of a merchant prince than a warrior king. His success in dealing in ivory, slaves and cloves brought prosperity to Zanzibar, earning him the title 'Said the Great'.

He was courteous and fair-minded, and in judicial matters was said to treat his sons and his slaves as equals.

The ruins of his first palace in Zanzibar, Mtoni, stand by the beach just north of the Stone Town. Tours of the ruins, and of other places that figured in the exceptional life of Princess Salme, one of Said's daughters, may be arranged through the nearby Mtoni Marine Centre.

▼ Below: A crucifix made from the wood of the tree under which Livingstone's heart was buried in 1857.

The Great Explorers and the Scramble for Africa

As slaves poured into Zanzibar during the third quarter of the 18th century, a succession of outstanding (if not always likable) men were heading in the opposite direction. It was the age of the **explorers**, when the nagging question of the source of the Nile was eventually 'settled' (by John Speke) and when giants of exploration and/or evangelical zeal – Krapf, Burton, Livingstone, Stanley, Grant, Thomson, Von der Decken and Teleki – strode out on their 'long walks'.

All these explorers passed through Zanzibar, which had continued to prosper under successive sultans, though their power dwindled as the British exerted diplomatic and military authority. Reluctantly, Sultan Barghash closed the slave market in Zanzibar in 1873, and soon afterwards, during the 'Scramble for Africa', the British made various treaties with Germany. They effectively took control in Zanzibar and much of what is now Kenya and Uganda, with most of present-day Tanzania, Rwanda and Burundi becoming **German East Africa**.

German rule was generally regarded as harsh. Its early years were marked by an Arab uprising along the coast, a war with the Hehe, and the Maji-Maji rebellion of 1905, in which the whole southern region united against their German overlords. All revolt was savagely suppressed, but the backlash against the Maji-Maji rebellion left the south devastated and 120,000 Africans dead. In Germany there was much disquiet about such brutality, although the Germans did do more to develop the country than their gentler successors, the British.

Tanganyika and Tanzania

In 1914 **World War I** came to East Africa. German-led forces, under their canny commander Von Lettow-Vorbeck, fell back before the British in a strategic retreat, keeping much-needed British manpower and resources from the Western Front. By the end of 1916, however, the British had established a provisional administration, and from 1922 the country, renamed Tanganyika, was governed by them under a League of Nations mandate.

◀ *Left: Former Sultan's Palace (now a museum) in Stone Town, Zanzibar Island.*

Zanzibar, Pemba and the coastal strip, however, remained in the possession of the Zanzibar sultanate.

By and large the British regarded Tanganyika as a poor relation of their adjacent colony, Kenya. Soon after World War II, the 'winds of change' began to blow and on 9 December 1961 the nation became independent, with **Julius Nyerere** at its head. Zanzibar's independence followed in December 1963 but a month later the last of its sultans was deposed in a bloody revolution. A few months after the revolution an arranged (and still troubled) marriage was convened between Zanzibar and Tanganyika, creating the United Republic of Tanzania. At the crux of the new republic was socialism, and the radical concept of *ujamaa*, derived from the Chinese Communist system of a village-based economy. Though Nyerere remained popular, his policies were less so, as Tanzania slid into severe economic depression, exacerbated by the break up of the East African Economic Community in 1977, and the war with Idi Amin's Uganda in 1978.

Nyerere stepped down as president in 1985. His successor, Ali Hassan Mwinyi, a Zanzibari, took over. In 1995 Tanzania became a multi-party democracy with Benjamin Mkapa as its president. Mkapa was re-elected in 2000 with Abeid Karume becoming president of Zanzibar (re-elected in 2005). Karume was succeeded by Ali Mohamed Shein (CCM) in 2010. President Jakaya Mrisho Kikwete (CCM) succeeded Benjamin Mkapa in 2005 (re-elected in 2010).

▲ *Above: Zanzibar State House, designed by British architect John Sinclair.*

Julius Nyerere was educated at a mission school near Lake Victoria, then went on to university in Uganda and Scotland. He became involved in politics on his return to Tanzania, and was at the forefront of movements towards independence. In 1961 he became Prime Minister of the new nation of Tanganyika, establishing his policy of *ujamaa*. Revered as the 'Father of the Nation', and widely known as *Mwalimu*, or teacher, many see him as a sincere but failed idealist. Tanzania's economy collapsed disastrously during his rule, but he did bestow some of his personal dignity upon his country and its people. He was a vocal opponent of repression in South Africa and elsewhere, and under him Tanzania, in a continent ravaged by war and tribalism, remained stable and peaceful. He died, still widely respected, in October 1999.

GOVERNMENT AND ECONOMY

From Independence in December 1961 until October 1995 Tanzania was a single-party state, its government elected by universal suffrage, from the age of 18 years. In 1977 the original mainland and Zanzibari factions merged to form the Revolutionary Party of Tanzania, Chama Cha Mapinduzi (CCM). The government was dedicated to the socialist ideals outlined in Julius Nyerere's Arusha Declaration (1967), much influenced by Mao Tse-tung's China.

When Nyerere stepped down from office in 1985 his successor, Ali Hassan Mwinyi, helped to bring about a shift from socialist idealism to a more pragmatic, relatively market-orientated style of government. This culminated, in 1995, in a multi-party system under Benjamin Mkapa, who continued the country's economic development, taken up, since 2005, by Jakaya Kikwete. In 2010 Kikwete was re-elected President for a second five-year term. In Zanzibar, Ali Mohamed Shein (CCM) has been proclaimed President of the Isles as head of a government of national unity (a coalition of CCM and opposition MPs). This coalition arrangement was agreed in advance in an attempt to avoid conflicts that in the past have threatened peace and security in Zanzibar, where the balance of power between CCM and CUF parties has been narrow and subject to challenge.

Economy

Various factors, among them radical socialism, poor management, corruption and the war with Idi Amin's Uganda contributed to Tanzania's economic collapse during the 1970s. Nyerere's well-intentioned policy of 'self-reliance' was seen to be over-ambitious, as his country relied even more extensively on overseas aid.

With Mwinyi's appointment (and among growing internal and external pressures for change) a shift of emphasis occurred, with a gradual liberalization of the economy and the privatization of inefficient parastatals and state-owned companies. Tanzania was still heavily dependent on outside aid but its economy was recovering. This was continued under Benjamin Mkapa. Mkapa kept Tanzania on course, despite many difficulties (including widespread corruption), earning the support of various international economists and governments. This progress is continuing under President Kikwete (re-elected in 2010).

Inflation has gradually risen from around 6% in 2002 to around 18% in 2012 and outside investment remains hampered by high taxation, corruption, bureaucracy and the slow implementation of reforms, but road and electronic communications continue to improve.

The economy still relies heavily upon agriculture, which provides around 85% of exports and employs some 80% of the work force, despite the fact that cultivated crops are limited, due to topographical and climatic conditions, to 4% of Tanzania's land area. Industry is primarily concerned with the processing of agricultural products, together with light consumer goods.

The country remains one of the world's poorest but prospects are brightening. Recent years have seen small improvements in industrial output and significant advances in mining, particularly gold. Substantial fields of natural gas are being found and developed offshore and there are still hopes of finding oil. Tourism, after suffering a few setbacks in the 1990s and early 2000s, has recovered well and continues to expand. With a 16% (approximately) share of the country's GDP it is an increasingly important contributor to Tanzania's economy. Meanwhile banking reforms have helped to improve private sector growth and Tanzania's GDP figures indicate a happier economic future for one of Africa's most deserving countries.

Natural Resources

Tanzania is not so much one of the world's poorest nations as one of its least developed. It is rich (if one includes its astonishing range of tourist attractions) in natural resources, among which are also gold, diamonds, gemstones (including Tanzanite – classed as a

TANZANIA IN NUMBERS

- **Population**: 46 million (expected to almost double by 2030).
- **Birth rate** per 1000 population: 32.8 (world average 27.1).
- **Death rate** per 1000 population: 11.6 (world average 9.9).
- **Life expectancy**: male 51.62 years; female 54.7 years.
- **Enrolment at Primary Schools**: 98%.
- **Enrolment at Secondary Schools**: 20%.

▼ Below: The fertile, sweeping upland and mountain areas which characterize Tanzania's Southern Highlands.

ROADS, TRAINS, PLANES AND FERRIES

- Tanzania still has many poor **roads** but most highways used by tourists are now surprisingly good. Many others are being upgraded.
- The **rail** network badly needs upgrading if it is to meet tourist standards. Journeys can be long, uncomfortable and frustrating, but the potential is considerable.
- After a disastrous privatization agreement and part-ownership by South African Airways, **Air Tanzania**, back under State control, is struggling to reassert itself as the national carrier. However, various private companies cover most internal tourist routes.
- **Ferries** operate on the great lakes and across certain rivers, and despite a few tragic accidents are generally reasonable. Ferries between Dar and the Zanzibar Islands run daily and are also generally fast, safe and reasonably comfortable.

precious stone), uranium, natural gas, nickel, iron, phosphates, hydropower and possibly oil. Cash crops include coffee, tea, cotton, sisal, tobacco, cloves, cashew nuts, pyrethrum and seaweed.

Health and Education

Health care is rudimentary in Tanzania. There are **hospitals** in all major towns and clinics in many villages but most are poorly equipped, though the best Tanzanian doctors have an excellent reputation. Malaria, AIDS, tuberculosis cholera and yellow fever are among the most serious diseases (tourists should not be over-concerned – *see* 'Health Precautions', page 125).

Schools are similarly poor in terms of resources and academic performance. Student teacher ratios are sometimes astonishingly high and teachers themselves poorly paid and often unmotivated. Attendance (among students and teachers alike) can be very erratic. Things are improving slowly and sincere attempts are being made to enhance that improvement but the general situation remains unsatisfactory. It will be some time before the extensive reforms now envisaged begin to bring about significant improvement.

Tourism

Tourism is now second to gold as a leading earner of foreign exchange but still brings in far more than agriculture, until recently the country's traditional mainstay.

Assuming that Tanzania maintains its well-established political, social and sectarian stability and that the present global recession does not continue for too long, the country's tourism industry should continue to expand at a steady rate.

Certainly Tanzania is blessed with remarkable natural and cultural attractions, many of which are still unknown to most outsiders.

▼ *Below: A hydrofoil ferry approaches Zanzibar.*

However, Tanzania's well-intended policy of 'high-cost/low-impact' tourism is slowly becoming 'high-cost/high-impact' in certain areas, and concerns are being raised about the increasingly expensive nature of tourism in the country. A more flexible system might need to be implemented, without compromising Tanzania's vulnerable heritage.

THE PEOPLE

There are 46 million Tanzanians, from more than 120 ethnic groups. No group is dominant and this, together with the Tanzanians' generally easy-going and tolerant nature and Julius Nyerere's non-factional ideals, has ensured continuing racial harmony. The relatively minor racial tensions are mainly between 'indigenous' and 'non-indigenous' citizens, 'non-indigenous' usually referring to people of Indian origin, though most 'local Asians' get on quietly with their lives and many work happily alongside 'indigenous' counterparts.

A greater concern, perhaps, is the Muslim/Christian situation. About 80% of Tanzania's population is fairly evenly divided between the two, and strains, exacerbated by political affiliations, sometimes show through. Most visitors, however, will remain unaware of any underlying unease, and find Tanzanians, of whatever religion or ethnic origin, friendly, peace-loving and very hospitable.

23%	Sukuma	6%	Gogo
18%	Swahili	6%	Ha
7.5%	Nyamwezi	4%	Kuramo
7%	Chagga	3%	Hehe
7%	Haya	1%	Maasai
7%	Makonde	10.5%	Others

THE TRIBAL GROUPS
OF TANZANIA

Ethnic Groups

It should be noted that the **Maasai**, fascinating and photogenic as they are, are not the only people in East Africa, and certainly not in Tanzania. 95% of native Tanzanians are actually of Bantu origin, rather than Nilo-Hamitic, and the Maasai are, as we have seen, only one of more than 120 ethnic groups.

▼ Below: Maasai elders in the Rift Valley.

▲ *Above: Datoga lady with baby, Lake Eyasi region.*
▶ *Opposite: A village near Lake Rukwa in southwestern Tanzania.*

The Maasai, of course, are undeniably attractive, and traditional pastoralist lifestyles are undoubtedly colourful. And as one of Tanzania's main tourist routes cuts across Maasailand these engaging people are hard to ignore.

But located between the Rift Valley and Ngorongoro is the fertile Mbulu Plateau, which most tourists also cross. It is home to the **Iraqw** (known as 'Mbulu' though they dislike the term). Not so immediately striking as their Maasai neighbours, the Iraqw, of Cushitic descent with fine-featured northern faces, are just as interesting. Unlike the Maasai they are cultivators as well as cattle herders.

A ninety-minute drive south of Ngorongoro, by the northern shores of Lake Eyasi, two most unusual peoples live side by side, in this dry, rocky country through which streams sometimes meander in swathes of welcome greenery. The **Datoga** are pastoralists and former enemies of the Maasai. Their 'warriors' are renowned lion killers, their girls sometimes so good looking, especially when dressed in traditional beaded leather, that they would, if they could tread the catwalks of London, Paris or New York, leave the western fashion world gasping.

Alongside them live the **Hadza** hunter-gatherers, perhaps the most interesting of all Tanzania's peoples. They eschew most 'civilized comforts' and do not build huts, preferring rudimentary shelters of natural vegetation, caves or even the bare earth. Sometimes they sleep in trees, like the baboons whose meat they prize more than any other. They use powerful longbows and poisoned arrows to bring down game as large as elephants and buffalo, but for most of the year live on wild berries, tubers, birds' eggs and honey. Naked but for simple shorts or aprons, sandals and a few beads, they might not seem unusual but they are.

Among the predominantly numerous Bantu groups are the **Sukuma**, Tanzania's largest tribe. They live around the southern and southeastern shores of Lake

Victoria, growing crops (including cotton) and keeping cattle. They are known especially for their expertise in drumming and for their snake dancing, which features huge pythons.

Other Bantu groups that tourists might encounter include the **Chagga**, who traditionally inhabit the lower slopes of Kilimanjaro and provide porters for the climb to the summit. But the sharp and enterprising Chagga are also to be found throughout Tanzania, wherever there is business to be done.

Visitors to Dar es Salaam will have the opportunity to meet the **Makonde**, in the Mwenge handicraft market (the actual Makonde homelands straddle the Tanzania/Mozambique border in the southeast). For the Makonde, expert stilt dancers, are better known for their fine wood sculptures, carved from African black-wood (commonly called ebony).

Travellers to the lovely Usambara Mountains will meet the gentle **Pare**, and around Dodoma on the central plateau the **Gogo**, who once resisted the Maasai. Tourists exploring the magnificent 'southern circuit' will encounter, near Iringa, the **Hehe** who resisted not only the Maasai but also the might of the colonial Germans. All are **Bantu**, of which there are more than a hundred other groups, all worthy of attention. One of the best ways to get to know them is via locally organized 'cultural tours'.

Village Life

The lifestyle of most Tanzanians is hard and limited, especially for women in the villages, who do much of the work as well as bearing and bringing up children. The birth rate is high and life expectancy low, although the latter is gradually improving. Villagers in particular spend much of their lives struggling to make ends meet; producing

THE MEN OF MAASAI

Traditional Maasai males:
● At the age of **four** or **five**, have two central lower incisors removed (to allow for feeding in case of lockjaw). They are given responsibility for the family's lambs, kids and calves.
● At the age of **six**, have their upper ear lobes pierced. Given responsibility for slightly older animals.
● At **puberty**, expected to undergo circumcision without anaesthetic.
● After an interim period, become junior warriors *ilmurran*; live with younger girls and the girls' mothers in a *manyatta* (warrior camp).
● At about **20**, become senior warriors.
● At about **27**, they become junior elders, and are allowed to marry.
● In their **30s**, join ranks of senior elders.
● In **old age**, cared for as *desati*, retired elders.
● On **death**, are put out in bush to be eaten by hyenas etc. Only distinguished elders and *loibons* (Maasai prophets) are buried.

THE MAKONDE CARVERS

Many Makonde moved into Tanzania from northeast Mozambique to avoid the ravages of war. These proud and highly sensitive people tend to isolate themselves in small groups and are regarded by other tribes with respect and sometimes a superstitious fear. Men and women file their teeth to points and adorn their faces and bodies with elaborate citracising, and the women wear large lip plugs made of metal. Their tribal ceremonies involve dancing, twisting and spinning on very high stilts, but they are best known for their 'ebony' carvings (actually African blackwood). Carvings are sold at the Mwenge Handicraft Market, in the northern suburbs of Dar es Salaam, and in curio shops in the tourist areas. The best carvings – often traditionally symbolic or abstracts of finely detailed family groups called ujamaa carvings – are unique, imaginative and quality works of art. There is, however, the usual mediocre stuff and 'touristy' souvenirs. Visitors should be prepared to take a long look around, and to haggle.

enough food (often with primitive tools), building huts, gathering fuel and fetching water. Life in the towns is, on the whole, seen as preferable (hence an increasing urban drift), though most people find that life is still a constant struggle to make ends meet.

Religion

Many rural people are animist, but most Tanzanians are Christian or Muslim. The Muslims, mostly living along the coast and in Zanzibar, represent about a third of the population, Christians about 45%. The small Asian communities are mostly made up of Hindus, Sikhs and several Muslim sects.

Sport and Recreation

The sporting passion among men and boys is **soccer** (football). Favourite teams are fervently supported in the large towns, and even in the villages boys will be seen kicking around a ball sometimes made of rags. **Boxing** and **wrestling** enjoy a minority following among the men, with **darts** being common in many bars and clubs. **Netball** is popular with women, and **volleyball** is sometimes played by both sexes.

▶ Right: Bao, a traditional game played with beans and a wooden board with cups scooped out of it, being played on Mafia island.

Water sports are not as popular with Tanzanians as one might expect in a country with a wonderful coastline and many lakes and rivers. Bilharzia (and sometimes hippos and crocodiles!) are a problem in freshwater lakes, though some people take an occasional dip in the sea.

Most Tanzanians love **music** and **dancing**, Zairean rhythms and bands being especially popular. And they love **conversation** (often sexually segregated, with urban, non-Muslim menfolk chatting in bars or clubs over a few bottles of lager, and in the villages in the shade of some tree, perhaps with a home-made brew). Tanzanians are avid readers of newspapers and listeners to radio broadcasts, and a small but increasing number now enjoy TV, videos and even the Internet.

▲ *Above: Worshippers on Zanzibar gather for a musical celebration at a Tarab festival.*

Food and Drink

The **staple** food throughout Tanzania is *ugali* – a stiff maize or cassava porridge. Beans, *mchicha* (a form of spinach) and bananas are also popular. **Meat** is generally too expensive for most Tanzanians to enjoy often. When affordable it usually comes in the form of *nyama choma* (roast meat), barbecued kebabs of goat meat or beef. Barbecued chicken is also a favourite. A stew of meat and plantains (*nyama na ndizi*) sometimes provides a tasty and nourishing alternative. Breakfast often involves deep fried doughnuts (*mandazi*) with tea (*chai*). The combination is appealing though tea (boiled Indian fashion with milk and sugar) might be too sweet for western tastes.

American/European cuisine is regular fare in hotels, lodges and restaurants, with a growing number of international restaurants in the cities and larger towns. A delicious array of tropical fruit is often presented, especially at breakfasts, in the better hotels.

Continental breakfasts are now common in tourist class hotels, though the British breakfast (minus pork products in some places in respect to Islamic obligations) fights a rearguard action. Lunches and dinners in such hotels, lodges and camps are almost invariably adequate and often excellent.

SEAFOOD

With the Indian Ocean as its eastern border Tanzania is a seafood lover's delight. Lobsters, prawns and calamari are readily available in most reputable hotels along the coast, and fish such as red or blue snapper, rock cod, sole, changu, and kingfish all make excellent eating. Lobster, garlic prawns or prawns *pili pili* (with a hot and spicy sauce), as well as various barbecued dishes are some of the local favourites.

2
Dar es Salaam and the Coast

Dar es Salaam is not particularly old or beautiful, but it is interesting and attractively situated. It has a disarming lack of pretension and its people, on the whole, are similarly casual and engaging, representing a colourful and cosmopolitan community.

Half-encircled by the waters of the **Indian Ocean**, Dar stands, or rather sleepily sprawls, midway down Tanzania's coastline. This coastal strip, 800km (500 miles) long, was once part of the medieval land of Zinj and the surprisingly advanced and enterprising Swahili civilization. It later became a fiefdom of the Zanzibari sultans, who sold it (under pressure) to the Germans during the 'Scramble for Africa'. The area is scattered with interesting ruins, such as those at **Kilwa**, formerly a famous and prosperous Swahili settlement. It is also a shoreline of some beauty, with many fine **beaches** and a sea teeming with fascinating marine life and, where the reefs have not been destroyed by 'dynamite fishing', ornamented with natural coral gardens.

Situated approximately 70km (45 miles) north of Dar es Salaam is **Bagamoyo**, whose clusters of Swahili-style homes and old buildings recall its 19th-century heyday when huge caravans bringing slaves and ivory from the interior, and explorers heading the other way, would pass through. Beyond Bagamoyo lies **Saadani National Park**, where big game can be found alongside the sea, and further north still are the drowsily pleasant little towns of **Pangani** and **Tanga**.

◀ *Opposite: Living palm and dying dhow; small symbols of a significant past on Bagamoyo beach.*

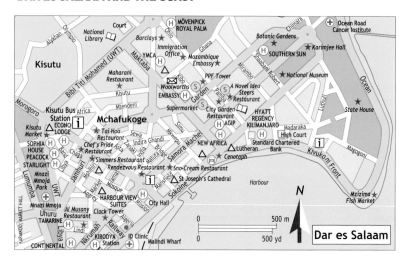

Dar es Salaam

DAR ES SALAAM

The inspiration behind Dar es Salaam was **Sultan Majid**, ruler of Zanzibar, who in 1866 began to build a palace on the mainland. His 'Haven of Peace' (as Dar es Salaam is commonly translated) was to have been his refuge from a troubled reign on the island, but Majid died in 1870 before his dreams could be fulfilled. His palace has gone, and all that remains of Majid's dreams is a fortified building, the Old Boma, on Sokoine Drive, and one other building nearby.

Seven years after Majid's death his 'Darra Salaam', according to one report, 'teemed with snakes, scorpions, centipedes, mosquitoes and other pests'. The **Germans**, seeking a deep-water harbour, shifted their headquarters down from Bagamoyo in 1891, and by 1914 they had built a railway from Dar to Lake Tanganyika, just in time for the British to take it over during World War I. Appropriately, the hostilities hardly disturbed the Haven of Peace, though the Royal Navy did lob a few shells shorewards, dislodging coconuts and damaging the old State House.

Dar es Salaam under German rule was an organized and pretty place. Even now Dar's shoreline is a pleasure to drive along, with its fine harbour and the blue seas and near-white sands which sweep around the northern suburbs. Like the Germans, the **British** erected various civic buildings and amenities, as well as bungalows and houses surrounded by lawns and gardens, though bougainvillea and hibiscus tended to proliferate rather than the honeysuckle and roses of home.

In places Dar es Salaam is still a refreshingly 'green' city, but is rapidly becoming less so. High-rise buildings are going up everywhere, roads are often badly congested and dangerous, and the population is increasing dramatically towards 5 million. However, the shops are fairly well stocked, and Dar is beginning to reflect a more dynamic, forward-looking Tanzania.

City Centre **

Dar es Salaam is an absorbing, laid-back mixture of east and west, old and new, races, tribes, religions and political philosophies; an all-pervading, often endearing miscellany of mankind. The city can be dirty, hot, humid and unsophisticated, and the traffic exasperating, but it is rarely boring, and most people who live there hold it in great affection. It is the country's main port and economic, cultural and political centre. No one seems to have told it that Dodoma, in central Tanzania, replaced it as the country's official capital some years ago.

◀ *Left: Flamboyant trees add a splash of colour to Dar es Salaam's otherwise unexceptional city centre.*

ASKARI MONUMENT

The Askari Monument pays tribute to the native troops who died in the 'Ice Cream War', the East African campaign during World War I, so called because the British were convinced that their German enemies would 'melt away like ice cream in the sun'. The monument (*askari* means 'soldier') has come to symbolize the sacrifice made by all the native African troops, in conflicts which were not of Africa's making, but World War I alone caused the deaths, directly or indirectly, of 100,000 of them. The inscription on the monument was composed by Rudyard Kipling.

To get to know Dar it is best to walk, at least around the central areas. The main focal point, in the middle of Samora Machel Avenue, is the **Askari Monument**. Southwest of the monument **Samora Machel Avenue** stretches away in an untidy bustle of pedestrians and traffic, the pavements cluttered with kiosks selling all manner of cheap goods and souvenirs. It is changing rapidly, with smart high-rise buildings replacing many older, dilapidated but often interesting lower structures. Luxury goods to be found in Dar's shops are imported, and visitors can usually buy the same things more cheaply back home. Local products can be disappointing but the better quality blackwood carvings, tinga-tinga paintings, basketry, shopping bags, Maasai beadwork, *khangas* (traditional cotton wraps) and (in Zanzibar) presentation packs of spices often represent good value. But newcomers to Dar will experience something of the city's easy-paced lifestyle, and something of its multicultural charm.

In the opposite direction Samora Machel heads towards the open sea, bypassing the **old Botanic Gardens** on one side, and the **National Museum** on the other. The gardens are quite pleasant. The National Museum con-

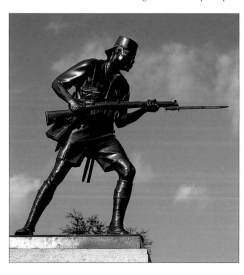

tains, among other important relics, the skull of 'Nutcracker Man' found by the Leakeys at Olduvai. There are also interesting displays of tribal artifacts and World War I memorabilia. The older part of the museum represents British colonial architecture of the period. Just a little way beyond the museum is **Karimjee Hall**, named after the Karimjees, one of Tanzania's notable old 'Asian' families, who donated the building to their adoptive country. The Hall is now used when parliament sits in Dar es Salaam (as opposed to Dodoma).

The seaward end of Samora Avenue terminates close to the **old German hospital**. It too is an interesting building, its lawns, baobabs and blossoming trees enlivening the stone solidity of the hospital itself. Its garden frontage offers a pleasant panorama of the sea and nearby shore.

▲ Above: The Old German Hospital still graces the seafront on Ocean Road.
◄ Opposite: One of Dar es Salaam's best-known landmarks, the Askari Monument.

Just to the south is the **State House**, with its own attractive lawns and trees. The official residence of the President, it is now screened by a wall and railings (photography is in any case forbidden). The British rebuilt it in 1922 from the ruins of its German forerunner, which was shelled during World War I. The original building was sensitively redesigned, its white-painted front acknowledging Islamic influences.

Kivukoni ★★

Beyond State House, where Ocean Road bends around towards Kivukoni Front, there is an interesting little corner of Dar. Here the visitor can explore the **fish market**, watch the ships and small dhows coming and going through the narrow **harbour** entrance, and at the same time observe a captivating spectrum of Dar es Salaam's population going about its business.

Beyond the fish market and ferry area the road, now Kivukoni Front, follows the curve of the harbour and offers views across the waterway on one side and the old German administration buildings, still in use, on the other. These buildings include, from east to west, the former Secretariat, High Court and German Officers' Mess. Further west stands the former Dar es Salaam Club and then the Lutheran Church (begun 1898), before the road merges with Sokoine Drive. Nearby is the Toyota Building (former German colonial home), followed by the former German Post Office, the White Fathers' House (1860s), St Joseph's Cathedral (begun 1897), the Old Boma (1860s), City Hall

SHOPPING IN DAR

In terms of variety and quality, Arusha is a better place than Dar for handicrafts and souvenirs. But among the better products available are:
- Makonde carvings;
- hand-woven basketwork;
- batiks, and the *kitenge* that are worn by most Tanzanian women;
- Maasai beadwork;
- Zanzibar chests – although they are expensive and shipping home would have to be arranged – and other Zanzibar antiques, such as silver necklaces and brooches;
- African music cassettes and CDs sold in most markets.

▶ Right: The rising edifice of St Joseph's Cathedral.

(German period) and the original German railway station.

Uhindini ('Indian Quarter') *

The area enclosed in the irregular square formed by Samora Machel Avenue and UWT Street, and Uhuru and Maktaba, roughly corresponds to the town's 'Indian quarter'. Here the visitor can absorb a distinctly Indian flavour – both in atmosphere and more literally, for there are places selling spicy snacks such as samosas, *bhajias* (chilli bites), or those eastern mysteries known as *paan*, normally chewed as a digestive after meals. The Asian communities have brought their own colour to the expanding city. Most of them are traders, shopkeepers or businesspeople, and their peace-loving, family-based cultures, whether Hindu, Muslim or Sikh, continue to contribute to that most attractive of Dar es Salaam's charms, its easy-going cosmopolitanism.

Among these streets it always pays to look up, as well as around. The mosques, temples, little rooms above the shops, and the clutter of tenement blocks almost always have something to offer: an ornate balcony, intricately fretworked stone screens, an Islamic motif worked into the beauty of a mosque and a thousand and one little glimpses into the day-to-day life among the extended Asian families. Above many doorways you will see a string of dead mango leaves, put up to bring good luck.

Kariakoo *

Another lively, crowded area, inhabited mostly by Africans, lies to the northwest of UWT Street. It is called Kariakoo. At its centre is a large market hall, but the sur-

---

DAR'S BEACHES

Oyster Bay beach is an attractive place, and in the late afternoons of weekends and public holidays, very popular with local Africans and Asians. The Coco Beach Restaurant and bar at its northern end is a main focal point, with more informal barbecue stands, ice cream, etc. a little way to the south. North of Dar, at Kunduchi, are other beaches, including **Bahari**, **Kunduchi** and **Whitesands**, but some of the beach resorts along Dar's southern coast, such as **Ras Kutani** and **Amani**, are better and more exclusive.

rounding streets are a bustling, rapidly developing matrix of traditional little *dukas* (shops) and new high-rise apartment blocks and business centres. The shops sell everything from plastic buckets and second-hand car spares to modern clothing and imported electronic goods.

Kariakoo gives visitors an insight into the fascinating diversity of Dar's ever-increasing African population, who mix easily but still maintain their own tribal customs and influences. Care must be taken as Kariakoo is off the beaten track for most tourists.

Northern Suburbs **

Hassan Mwinyi Street leads out of town to the north, and along it are three other noteworthy buildings: the *Nyumba ya Sanaa*, or **House of Art**, where visitors can buy a variety of African artifacts such as woven baskets, mats and batiks, the **Greek Orthodox Church** (in Romanesque Basilican style) and the **Ismaili Jama'at Khana**. The latter is a religious community centre for Ismaili Muslims. A little way to the north of Selander bridge by Haile Selassie Road is **St Peter's Roman Catholic Church**, with its perforated screens and barrel-vaulted roof, and the **Little Theatre Club**, which normally has a lively repertoire, advertised in the local media.

Seaward are the relatively leafy suburbs of **Oyster Bay**. The bay itself is pretty especially in late afternoon, or under a full moon. Toure Drive, which follows the seafront, continues to Msasani Peninsula. There are three hotels overlooking the sea along this route, the Oyster Bay, the Golden Tulip and the Sea Cliff. The Sea Cliff has an adjoining shopping mall where you will find restaurants and fast-food outlets. There

▼ *Below:* Nyumba ya Sanaa, the House of Art, near the Dar es Salaam Mövenpick (Royal Palm) Hotel.

▲ Above: Oyster Bay is particularly pretty in the late afternoon.

is also a smaller precinct across the road.

By Msasani Bay, on the western side of the peninsula, is the beautifully situated Dar es Salaam Yacht Club and the Slipway Plaza, which has shops, souvenir stalls and restaurants. Each shopping precinct includes a supermarket and there are banks (Standard Chartered and Barclays respectively) at the Seacliff and Slipway.

Skirting the Msasani Peninsula to the west, the Bagamoyo Road carries on north passing the **Village Museum**, an authentic collection of traditional style huts, and the **University**, set on a low hill. Close to the university is the large **Milimani Shopping Mall** and nearby **Mwenge Handicraft Market**, famous for its Makonde carvings. About 24km (15 miles) north of Dar es Salaam is **Kunduchi**, the main beach resort on this part of the coast, and the site of some Arab ruins.

KUNDUCHI RUINS

Just inland from Kunduchi Village and adjacent to it are some early Arab tombs among the baobabs and coastal scrub. They are fine examples of their type, with unique pillars inscribed with Islamic chronologies and porcelain bowls set in the pillars. The delicate pottery bespeaks a fine life style among the coastal Arabs of the period, and with bowls from China and England, indicates the extent of the coast's worldwide trade links.

BAGAMOYO

Bagamoyo is now easily accessible from Dar, though the road can be congested in its southern sector. The small town, 70km (45 miles) from Dar, gives the impression of having slept through the 20th century. Its name is said to mean 'Here I lay down my heart', probably deriving from the relief and joy of the caravan leaders and porters rather than the despair of any accompanying slaves, whose hearts must have given up beating (metaphorically) long before.

History

As a terminal point on the coast for Arab trading caravans, Bagamoyo naturally became a holding depot for **slaves** brought from the interior. Most slaves were shipped to Zanzibar crammed into dhows. About half of

them were kept in Zanzibar to work on the clove plantations and elsewhere. The rest were dispersed, under terrible conditions, to Arabia, Persia and Southeast Asia.

Famous explorers also passed through Bagamoyo.
Among them were the brilliant **Burton** and the more
taciturn **Speke**, who was soon, during his second
expedition with Grant, to settle the age-old question
of the Nile. In 1871 **H.M. Stanley**, with 192 men and
six tonnes of equipment, strode off at his usual headlong
pace to look for David Livingstone. He returned the
following year in triumph, though at 31 his hair had
turned grey and he was 'fearfully worn'.

Stanley last stayed in Bagamoyo for one eventful night
in 1889, when his party (reduced to 196 from an original
708) marched into town after a three-year expedition
across the continent. With him was **Emin Pasha**, governor
of Equatoria, whom Stanley had rescued from the 'mad
Mullah's' hordes. The Germans threw a lavish party at
their headquarters (which still exists) to celebrate the
return of the explorers. Emin, short-sighted and perhaps
made unsteady by champagne, fell from an upper window and fractured his skull. 'The Pasha', in the words of
Evelyn Waugh, 'had taken a header off the balcony'.

LIVINGSTONE'S RETURN

David Livingstone died as he
knelt in prayer in a village hut
in what is now eastern Zambia.
His faithful Zanzibari servants
Abdulla Susi and James Chuma
cut out his heart, buried it
under a tree, and then took
nine months to help carry his
sun-dried remains, enwrapped
in bark, to the coast. On arrival
in Bagamoyo, the men laid
down their burden outside the
Mission Church, where they
announced: 'Mwili wa Daudi'
– 'The body of David'. The tale
of that journey from the interior
is one of the most moving
stories in the annals of African
exploration. By one of those
ironies that seem inevitable
in Africa, the body, in a new
coffin of zinc and wood, was
transported from Bagamoyo
to Zanzibar on board *HMS
Vulture*, before it was taken
to London and buried in
Westminster Abbey. The dour
Scots missionary, not without
humour, would have appreciated the joke.

◀ *Left: The unpretentious
streets of a once-important
terminus of the slave and
ivory trade, Bagamoyo.*

EMIN PASHA

Born Eduard Schnitzer to Jewish parents in Prussian Silesia, Emin joined the Turkish army, and was later appointed governor of the Egyptian province of Equatoria (roughly modern Sudan). When the Arabs turned on him, he was rescued by Stanley, and during the celebrations for their safe return to Bagamoyo in 1889 the Pasha, of poor sight and a little tipsy, fell from a window of the German headquarters. He recovered from his fractured skull but less than two years later, sitting at a table in his tent in the Congo peering at his beloved specimens of animals and plants, Arab slave traders strolled in and unceremoniously cut his throat.

Around Town

Bagamoyo itself is a nondescript collection of *dukas* (small shops) and huts, with a few larger buildings here and there. Some of the shops and houses have elaborately carved doors. Places worthy of note include the old **caravanserai**, the Sewa Haji School, the former **German headquarters** (there are two), and Bagamoyo's oldest building, a fortified **Arab house** begun in 1860. Used at one time as a pen for slaves awaiting shipment, it became a military garrison in German times and a prison under the British. The **Bagamoyo College of Arts**, just to the south of the town, is also worth visiting. A string of pleasant resorts lines the beach just to the north of town.

Mission ★★

Close to these beach resorts stands the first Catholic Mission in East Africa, built in 1868 by the Fathers of the Holy Ghost. Originally intended to house children rescued from slavery, it expanded to become a church, a school, and a collection of workshops and farming projects. It was to this mission that Livingstone's body was brought in 1874.

The Mission remains much as it was then. The old buildings and a museum are the main attractions, but visitors might be interested to know that many exotic plants

▶▶ *Opposite: Swahili ruins at Kaole, near Bagamoyo.*
▶ *Right: The Fathers' House at Bagamoyo's historic Catholic Mission.*

which now grace the streets and gardens of Tanzanian cities were first introduced here. Coffee was also planted.

The Kaole Ruins **

Five kilometres (3 miles) south of Bagamoyo are the Kaole ruins. They are basically medieval, though some structures (including the West Mosque, once perhaps the finest on the mainland) date back to the 13th and 14th centuries AD. Kaole was once the main coastal trading centre between Kilwa and Mombasa, though like other towns of Zinj it declined with the coming of the Portuguese. Among its other notable buildings are a 15th-century house and some double 'love graves', which speak of the prosperous life (and death) styles that merchants enjoyed at the height of the Swahili civilization.

Saadani National Park *

Gazetted in 2005 as Tanzania's 13th national park, Saadani is also the only East African game sanctuary bordered by the sea. Now almost 1000km² (386 sq miles) in area it embraces a wide variety of habitats, which support an eclectic collection of animal and bird species, including at least 24 large mammals. Among these is the rare Roosevelt sable antelope. Green turtles breed on one of the beaches (Madete) and whales pass through the adjacent Zanzibar Channel in October and November. In the dry season, away from the Wami River, water is scarce and animals less numerous, but the reserve is always worth visiting, except during heavy rains. In Saadani Village, 50km (30 miles) north of Bagamoyo, there is an old German fort and some German graves. Saadani Safari Lodge, close to the village, organizes game drives and boat trips up the Wami River.

THE BAGAMOYO CATHOLIC MISSION

In 1914 the peace of Bagamoyo was disturbed when the British mounted a naval bombardment and air attack on the town. As the Mission was left unmolested, the Germans moved most of their troops into its grounds, among the coconut palms that still flourish between the Mission buildings and the shore. Rather touchingly, they took three ancient, ornamental cannons from the Mission gardens and placed them among their more realistic defence battery. The British were neither fooled by the cannon nor deterred by the Mission's neutrality. They pounded the seafront and the coconut palms, damaging the Fathers' House and the new church. Miraculously 2000 civilians sheltering in the Mission were unhurt. The German positions were soon overrun by a landing party and the garrison was taken.

▲ *Above: Relics of once prosperous lifestyles, at Tongoni, by Tanga.*

BEES IN THEIR BONNETS

Sleepy little Tanga was the site of a fierce battle in 1914, when the British landed an 8000-strong assault force, mostly Indian troops, in an attempt to capture the Tanga railway line. Unfortunately the canny German commander, Von Lettow-Vorbeck, was given time to muster his forces. As the queasy assault force hit the beaches and struggled through the bush towards the town with bullets whipping around their turbans, they were attacked by a swarm of bees. It was more than enough for the attackers, who made a hasty retreat, leaving much of their equipment and morale behind. Some divisions took more casualties from the bees than the bullets, although the bullets proved more deadly, killing 800 and wounding 500.

TANGA AND PANGANI

Tanga port stands some 230km (140 miles) north of Dar. Its main street, along which troops of vervet monkeys sometimes roam, has an air of dilapidated colonial provincialism, but the town is a relaxing stopping-off point between Dar and Mombasa, and for dhows crossing from the harbour to Pemba Island.

For a brief time capital of German East Africa, **Tanga** remains one of the larger towns in the country, though with the decline in the sisal industry its economy is in urgent need of revival. There are various places of interest, including the **Amboni Caves**, with limestone formations and colonies of fruit bats, the **Galanos Sulphur Springs** and the **Tongoni Ruins**, as well as some pleasant beaches. It is also possible to drive into the Usambara Mountains from the village of Muheza to **Amani** Nature Reserve, a most attractive area rich in endemic birds and plants.

Pangani, on the estuary of the river of the same name and 45km (28 miles) south of Tanga, offers similarly quiet charms. It had fewer charms for the Arab rebel Abushiri, one of the leaders of an anti-German revolt, who was hanged here in 1897, but present-day visitors might enjoy the waterfront and there are a few interesting buildings, including an Arab fort and some old slave-traders' mansions. There are some very attractive little beach resorts close to Pangani, well worth a short detour for anyone passing through the area.

SOUTH OF DAR

Immediately to the south of Dar es Salaam, across the Kivukoni ferry, are some beautiful beaches and some pleasant resorts, among which are Ras Kutani and Amani. Beyond the beaches immediately south of Dar es Salaam, the coast is still largely undeveloped, its shoreline broken only by the watery maze where the Rufiji slides into the sea.

Kilwa *

One hundred kilometres (60 miles) south of the Rufiji Delta is the once-important settlement of Kilwa. Or rather the three Kilwas – Kilwa Kivinje and Kilwa Masoko, on their mainland peninsula, and the small island settlement of Kilwa Kisiwani. It is difficult nowadays to believe that the Kilwas thrived on gold, slaves and ivory from the the 12th century, when it was first settled by Gulf Arabs, until the 1860s, when something like 20,000 slaves a year were shipped to servitude from its mangrove swamps. As early as 1502, when Vasco da Gama sailed in, an estimated 12,000 'black Moors' were living there.

Kilwa Kivinje retains features of its old Arabic and colonial German associations, and **Kilwa Masoko** still flourishes, though the market from which it gets its name has nothing to do with slaves. But it is mostly the island of **Kilwa Kisiwani** which tourists and travellers seek out, for the ruins there represent the most exceptional examples of early Islamic architecture in sub-Saharan Africa.

The Far South

Tanzania's southeastern coast has been shaken from its slumbers by the discovery of large natural gas fields offshore, Mtwara being the exploration companies' base. But this little-known area also offers secluded beaches, diving, snorkelling, fishing and a few places of historical interest. Off Mikindani lies the Mnazi Bay-Ruvuma Estuary Marine Park and, within striking distance, the promising Luwika-Lumesule Game Reserve. Livingstone's old house, and an old German Boma (now a hotel), can be seen in Mikindani.

THE KILWA RUINS

Here are some highlights of the outstanding ruins on Kisiwani Kilwa:
- The magnificent **Great Mosque**, beautiful even in decay. Built in the 12th century, it was partly reconstructed in the 15th.
- Close by is the **Small Domed Mosque**. This, with its dome surmounted by a unique octagonal tower and its vaults once adorned by porcelain bowls, is perhaps the best-preserved of the island's ruins.
- One of the most impressive of the old buildings is **Husina Kubwa**, which commands a fine view across the straits from its vantage point on a projecting cliff. Husina means 'fort' in Arabic, but the building is thought to have been the palace of a wealthy ruler.
- There is a fort on the island, the **Gereza**, which dominates the northern shores. It was built by Omani Arabs in the early 19th century, on the foundations of a Portuguese stronghold.

BEST TIMES TO VISIT

The coast is best from mid-May to mid-October. Jan–Mar can be uncomfortably hot and humid, but monsoon breezes often temper the air. Rain in Mar–Apr, and to a lesser extent Nov–Dec, can sometimes be heavy and frustrating.

GETTING THERE

International airlines now fly directly to and from the Julius Nyerere Airport in Dar es Salaam (tel: 022 284 2402) and Kilimanjaro Airport (Moshi/Arusha, tel: 027 255 4252).

GETTING AROUND

Most visitors who fly within Tanzania use **charter companies**, including: Coastal Aviation (tel: 075 262 7825), Precision Air (tel: 022 286 0701) and Zanair (Zanzibar, tel: 024 223 2857). **Long-distance buses** run (often recklessly!) between most major towns and cities. Dar Express is among the better ones. **Rail travel** is possible (to the southwest, west and north) but not recommended. **Ferries** connect Dar Harbour with Zanzibar Town, taking 1½ hours or less. Companies include Azam Marine (tel: 022 213 4013), Sea Express, (tel: 022 213 7049) and Sea Star (tel: 022 213 9996). **Travel/safari companies** operate in most urban areas. **Car hire** isn't cheap but services are improving. **Taxis** are cheap but haggling is advised; fees should be agreed before departure.

WHERE TO STAY

Among the better hotels in a generally not-too-impressive range are:

Dar es Salaam

Southern Sun, tel: 022 213 7575, www.tsogosunhotels.com Mid-upper range, one of Dar's best options, pleasant central location.

Oyster Bay Hotel, tel: 0193 226 0618, reservations@the oysterbayhotel.com Up-market hotel with pleasant gardens and pool, by popular Oyster Bay, northern suburbs.

Hyatt Regency Kilimanjaro, tel: 0764 701 234, daressalaam. kilimanjaro@hyatt.com www. daressalaam.kilimanjaro.hyatt. com Five-star hotel overlooking Dar harbour.

Sea Cliff, tel: 022 260 0380, www.hotelseacliff.com Luxury hotel near tip of Msasani Peninsula, attractive location. Adjacent to small shopping mall with various cafés and restaurant outlets.

Atlantis Hotel, tel: 022 266 4591-4, info@atlantishotel. co.tz www.atlantishotel.co.tz Northern suburbs. Pleasant mid-range stylish hotel.

Slipway Hotel, tel: 022 260 0893, slipway@coastal.cc www.slipway.net Mid-range accommodation by popular waterside shopping/leisure centre, northern suburbs.

Beach Hotels Near Dar

NORTHERN

Mediterraneo, tel: 022 261 8359, www.mediterraneo tanzania.com By Msasani Bay, northern suburbs, restaurant.

Kunduchi Beach, tel: 022 265 0050/1, info@kunduchi.com www.kunduchi.com Recently upgraded, 24km north of Dar city centre.

Jangwani Seabreeze, tel: 022 264 7215, gmjangwani@ eclipsehotelsafrica.com www. jangwaniseabreezeresort.com Beach hotel 20km north of Dar centre. Three pools, games room, tennis, go-karts.

SOUTHERN

Ras Kutani, tel: 022 212 8485, info@selous.com www.selous.com Probably best (mid-range/luxury) beach resort close to Dar.

Bagamoyo Beach Resorts

Traveller's Lodge, tel: 023 244 0077, info@travellers-lodge.com www.bagamoyo. com/travellers-lodge Best of Bagamoyo's beach resorts.

Saadani NP

Saadani Safari Lodge, tel: 071 355 5678, reservations@ saadanilodge.com www. saadani.com Only lodge inside Saadani NP, by beach.

Tanga and Pangani

The Tides Lodge, tel: 078 422 5812, info@thetideslodge. com www.thetideslodge.com Best beach resort in the area. Just south of Pangani.

Kilwa

Kilwa Ruins Lodge, tel: 022 213 3864, info@kilwaruins lodge.com www.kilwaruins lodge.com Mid-range beach lodge at Kilwa Masoko, specializing in sports fishing.

Kimbilio Lodge, tel: 065 602 2166, www.kimbiliolodges.com Mid-range beach lodge, Kilwa Masoko. Scuba, sports fishing, game-viewing excursions, trips to Kilwa ruins.

Mtwara
The Old Boma, tel: (Mtwara) 078 436 0110, oldboma@mikindani.com www.mikindani.com Former German Fort. Excursions to Lukwika-Lumesule Game Reserve, nearby Mzazi Bay Marine Reserve.

WHERE TO EAT

Restaurants in Dar can be inconsistent and disappointing but better ones include:

Southern Sun Hotel (by the Botanic Gardens, city centre) has two: **Kivulini Restaurant** (continental) and **Baraza Grill** (grills, tapas, etc.).
Hyatt Regency Kilimanjaro Hotel (town centre) has two up-market restaurants: **Oriental** (far eastern) and **The Palm** (international). Pricey but good, the latter is noted for its Sunday brunches.
Zuane (Msaseni Peninsula). Probably the best Italian food in Dar.
Karambezi Restaurant (Seacliff Hotel) has recently been extended and improved.
George and Dragon (Msasani Peninsula). English. Excellent fish and chips/Sunday roasts, smoking allowed.
Addis in Dar (northern suburbs). Ethiopian.
Coral Ridge Spur (Seacliff Village). Steak and chips, Mexican food, etc.

Mediterraneo (northern suburbs, on the beach).
Epid'or (Msasani peninsula). This Lebanese/French café/restaurant is a popular spot.
Osaka (Oyster Bay). Japanese/Korean.
Alcove (Seacliff Hotel). Indian/Chinese.

Popular, less formal options
Mashua Waterfront (Slipway, Msasani). Here you can have fish, chicken, steaks, etc., often accompanied with glorious sunsets across adjacent Msasani Bay.
Black Tomato (Msasani Peninsula, also at Novel Idea Bookshop, Oyster Bay). Pleasantly low-key cafés.
Mamboz (town centre). Barbecued chicken/meat.
Shahi Darbar (Msasani Peninsula). Pakistani barbecued chicken/meat, etc.

TOURS AND EXCURSIONS

Tours of Dar: *See* local magazine *Advertising Dar*, available at supermarkets and bookshops.
Boat trips to Bongoyo Island: Boats leave from the Dar Slipway, Masaki.
Excursions to Zanzibar and other islands: Zanzibar Town is just 1½ hours away from Dar es Salaam by ferry so

return day trips are quite feasible, though it is better to stay for a few days. Mafia and Kilwa can be reached by scheduled flights.
Safaris from Dar: Various Dar-based safari companies do short trips to Mikumi, Saadani or the Selous wildlife sanctuaries and safaris further afield.
Bagamoyo: Bagamoyo is only 1½ hours' drive north of Dar, though an overnight stay at a beach resort (like Traveller's Lodge) is recommended.
Bird walks around Dar: *See* latest copy of *Advertising Dar* (*see* above) for details.
Entertainment Parks: 'Wet and Wild' and 'Water World' (water parks, both a 30–40 minute drive north of Dar).
Dar Zoo and **Fun City** are both reached by crossing on the Kigamboni ferry.

USEFUL CONTACTS

Code for Dar: 022
Code for Tanga: 027
Code for Lindi/Mtwara: 023
Police/Fire/Ambulance: tel: 111, 112 or 999.
Dar es Salaam International Airport: 022 284 2402.
Aga Khan Hospital: Head of patients care, tel: 022 211 5151/3.
TMJ Hospital, tel: 022 270 007/8.

DAR ES SALAAM	J	F	M	A	M	J	J	A	S	O	N	D
AVERAGE TEMP. °F	81	81	81	79	75	75	75	75	75	77	79	81
AVERAGE TEMP. °C	27	27	27	26	26	26	26	26	26	25	26	27
RAINFALL in	2	3	4	11	9	1	1	1	1	2	3	3
RAINFALL mm	49	75	114	289	216	25	27	24	37	63	73	83
DAYS OF RAINFALL	3	5	9	18	13	4	4	5	6	6	6	9

3
The Land of Kilimanjaro

'As wide as all the world, great, high and unbelievably white in the sun. . . .' For a writer who made the adjective an endangered species, four in one sentence is a rare extravagance. Hemingway, we can safely assume, was impressed by Kilimanjaro.

With good reason, for the mountain he describes is remarkably beautiful. And the land over which it rises, in such imposing isolation, is scarcely less so. To the west, beyond farms and fields of coffee, the dark pyramid of **Mount Meru** towers above **Arusha National Park**. Beyond Meru a volcanic landscape sweeps up to the Kenyan border and down towards the **Rift Valley**.

South of the two great mountains stretches the so-called Maasai Steppe, with **Tarangire National Park** in its northwest corner, while southeast of Kilimanjaro the **Pare Mountains** diminish towards the coast in a pleasing swirl of hills, valleys, and eventually savanna, much of it enclosed in one of Tanzania's loveliest game sanctuaries, **Mkomazi**. The Pare ranges are continued south by the **Usambaras**, rich in endemics and scenic splendour.

The two towns found in the region are small, but both are of significance to most visitors. **Moshi**, the quiet, strangely pious centre of the Chagga homelands, stands closest to Kilimanjaro on the mountain's lower southern slopes. Its more secular counterpart and tourist capital of the region, **Arusha**, lies below Meru. Until recently Arusha exuded a frontier-town functionality, its unpretentious shops just as likely to sell clutch plates as to

CLIMATE

The dry months from June to October are cool, especially in the evenings and early mornings, when the mean temperature drops to 15°C (59°F). Daytime temperatures, even in the dry season, can be quite hot on the plains, but humidity is low compared with the coast. The wettest months are March and April, when some park tracks can be impassable, with a shorter rainy season mid-October to mid-December.

◀ *Opposite: Kibo peak, Kilimanjaro's (and Africa's) highest point.*

45

deal in curios, but it is developing quickly into a much larger, more dynamic city. The city centre is often plagued by touts and is losing much of its former small-town charm.

KILIMANJARO ***
History and Background

Many tourists arrive in the north of Tanzania at Kilimanjaro International airport. If they land by daylight they will usually be treated to a spectacular view of a most spectacular mountain, which dominates, physically and figuratively, the entire plains from which it rises. Thought to be dormant rather than dead, Kilimanjaro is young in geological terms, having been created during massive eruptions about 750,000 years ago.

Despite the fact that the area of its base is larger than that of Greater London, and that it is said to be the highest free-standing mountain in the world, Kilimanjaro remained unknown to the west until 11 May 1848. On that day the German missionary **Johannes Rebmann**, armed with his Bible and umbrella, fancied he saw, on the summit of one of the 'mountains of Jagga' (as he called the three clouded peaks of Kilimanjaro), a 'dazzling white cloud'. His guide laconically told him that the cloud was *baridi* – cold. Rebmann realized that what he was looking at was snow.

▶ Opposite: Kilimanjaro National Park headquarters, the starting point for ascents up the mountain by the Marangu route. The park has recently been extended to more than double its previous size.

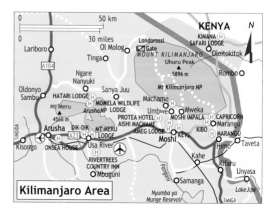

Kilimanjaro Area

His reports were ridiculed by distinguished geographers back in England. The idea of a snow-topped mountain just south of the equator seemed absurd, but the gentle missionary was of course right. It was over 40 years before another German, **Dr Hans Meyer**, and an alpine guide, **Ludwig Purtscheller**, became the first men to climb the loftiest of the great mountain's three peaks, Kibo, at 5896m (19,340ft) the highest point in Africa

The **Chagga** who live on its slopes have no word for the mountain which is at the centre of their lives, only for its two main peaks, Kibo and Mawenzi. No-one really knows how Kilimanjaro got its popular name, but ironically the word *Kilima* in Kiswahili means hill rather than mountain. Perhaps the diminutive was used out of familiarity, for Kilimanjaro (or 'Kili', to many) seems to inspire affection. The famous 'Christmas pudding' mountain is instantly familiar all over the world, often (ironically) from photographs taken from Amboseli National Park in Kenya. Its popularity is enhanced by the fact that many thousands of visitors reach the summit each year, and Kili can justifiably claim to be the highest mountain in the world accessible to non-expert mountaineers. Truly a mountain of the people.

THE CHAGGA

To the Chagga the importance of Kilimanjaro cannot be over-emphasized. The mountain gives them shelter and its slopes sustenance, but above all it gives them an identity: an old, precise, deep-rooted sense of place. A Bantu-speaking race, visitors will meet them as guides and porters on Kili, and they are considered one of the most enterprising, forward-looking people in Tanzania. One feature of their culture is that their language is rich in place names. The most ordinary stream will have a name of its own, helping to place it in the mental maps and the 'tribal memory' of the local people, and incidentally reflecting the importance of water to a people who can see, from their mountain home, the dust-storms blowing across the baked red earth of the plains below.

Moshi *

Moshi stands on the lower southern slopes of Kilimanjaro, but it is often bypassed on the way to the start of the climb at Marangu. The town has a wonderfully picturesque setting, but is respectable rather than exciting. The international airport is 34km (21 miles) to the west, and the town is also accessible by rail and road. Arusha, an hour's drive to the west of Moshi, is the nearest sizeable centre, while a further three hours' drive to the north and into Kenya is Nairobi, a well-established tourist centre.

THE LAND OF KILIMANJARO

Some of the most commonly related of Kilimanjaro's tales are those of altitude sickness. Even the fittest athlete can succumb to this humiliating and unpleasant illness, and popular though climbing Kili is, it is not something to be undertaken lightly.
• The effects of altitude sickness start around 3500m (10,500ft). The symptoms are a loss of appetite, sleeplessness, headaches, nausea and fatigue.
• The best ways to deal with it are to take plenty of liquid, carbohydrate and sleep when you can, to climb *pole pole* (slowly), and to spend a second night at Horombo hut acclimatizing. If things get really bad, descend. It's an instant cure.
• Other dangers on the mountain are the severe cold on the summit, which demands proper equipment (it can be hired from Marangu), and the sun, which many forget about.
• There is a mountain rescue team on the mountain. Everyone climbing the mountains pays a rescue fee to cover this service.

The village of **Marangu**, half an hour's drive east of Moshi, is the starting point for most ascents of the mountain. A number of operators are based here, as well as the area's two oldest hotels, the Kibo and the Marangu. Newer hotels and guest houses are appearing. Marangu is a pleasant village with an alpine feel, and lies 7km (4 miles) from the entrance to the National Park gate, which marks the start of the most popular tourist route up Kilimanjaro.

Climbing Kilimanjaro ★★

From Marangu, at 1500m (5000ft), the mountain can look overwhelmingly high, but would-be climbers have little to fear except the unpleasant effects of altitude sickness. Tens of thousands of people climb Kili every year, and tens of thousands come safely down again. Most people opt for the standard five-day climb, though some people choose to spend an extra night at the second of the trail's three huts, to help acclimatize.

Day One: The first stage of the climb is through the rain forest, a lovely three- or four-hour trek from the park entrance to the first complex of A-frame huts, named after the famous Chagga chief **Mandara**, at 2700m (8850ft). The forest zone, which girdles the mountain, is the second of

▶ *Right: In the dank, sultry air of the rainforest at the start of the climb, the snow and ice of the summit seems a long way away.*

◀ *Left: Day one of the climb, through the forest zone.*

the five distinctive vegetative zones walkers experience on their ascent. It has a characteristic rainforest atmosphere; a damp, green luxuriance which for some people is claustrophobic. Among the mighty trees, festooned with vines and lichens, Sykes or Colobus monkeys are sometimes seen, as is the brilliant crimson flash of a Hartlaub's turaco. As the path approaches Mandara Hut one encounters the first groves of giant heather.

Day Two: After an overnight stop at Mandara, walkers press on (or more wisely saunter) to the second complex of huts at **Horombo**, at 3720m (12,200ft). Skirting Maundi Crater to the west, the track climbs a fairly steep and sometimes slippery bank of rainforest, soon emerging on to the heathland zone, which in turn becomes upland moors. This is beguiling country of open views and muted moorland colours, where modest but beautiful plants abound. The plants are tougher than they look, and it is easy for the walker to forget that this gentle, rolling country is higher than the peaks of the Pyrenees. *Pole pole* is the order of the day, for the last few kilometres of the five-hour walk to Horombo involves some small but deceptively tiring ravines.

Climbing Kilimanjaro can seem a bit of a dawdle these days, but getting there first was a bit more daunting.

● In 1861 the German explorer **Von der Decken** attempted Kilimanjaro but saw off his celebratory magnum of champagne (and his chances of reaching the summit) long before he emerged from the foothills.

● Sixteen years later Hungarian bon viveur **Count Samuel Teleki** and his companion paid similar respects to a bottle of red wine as they camped in the snow on The Saddle. They got little further.

● In 1889, **Hans Meyer** and **Ludwig Purtscheller** reached the crater rim after an exhausting climb over the crevasse-ridden icecap. Weakened and wearied they staggered back to camp, but the next morning (3 October) they returned, eventually reaching the highest point in Africa. Meyer planted a small German flag, the two men shook hands, raised three cheers for their Kaiser, and called the peak Kaiser Wilhelm Spitze – now Uhuru (Freedom) Point.

Day Three: Just after Horombo climbers pass a stream known ominously as Last Water then some low, striated cliffs known as Zebra Rocks. Ahead is the Saddle, the sway-backed ridge which connects Kilimanjaro's two main peaks, **Kibo** and **Mawenzi**. Beyond Zebra Rocks the track forks. The path to the right is the more direct route to the Saddle, the gradual path to the left the more frequently recommended route. Whatever route is taken, the Saddle is not a welcoming place. The five- or six-hour walk is quite gentle, but the last upcurve to **Kibo Hut**, at 4700m (15,400ft), can turn legs to sandbags and make hearts go into overdrive.

Days Four and Five: Kibo Hut is a dreary place at the best of times, with an atmosphere as congenial as a condemned cell in Siberia. Walkers huddle into sleeping bags, not to sleep but to keep warm. Heads pounding, stomachs churning, they wait to be dragged out, at 01:00 or 02:00, into the icy darkness. Then, with a guide leading the way holding a small lantern, each party files into the night up the steep, zigzag track which leads to **Gillman's Point** on the summit crater rim. The early start allows walkers to reach Gillman's by dawn and to see the spectacular sunrise beyond Mawenzi and, with the scree freezing at night, provides a safer footing. But the third

▶ *Right: Kibo peak looms large for climbers on the Mweka route.*

reason for making this final ascent in darkness is to maintain a visual ignorance; if walkers could see what lies ahead, how steep the slope is, how high above them the rocks were that mark the last scramble to the rim, they might well lose heart and turn back.

And so they plod on, mountain sticks tapping out a slow, staccato rhythm. The guide sometimes sings a plaintive song, to placate the mountain, and to take the minds of his charges off their ordeal. At this altitude, oxygen is twice as rare as at sea level; breathing becomes laborious, paced steps and frequent stops are important. Almost every step becomes an effort of will. Halfway to Gillman's Point (and about two hours above Kibo Hut) is an overhang known as Hans Meyer cave, in which walkers often take a breather.

Above the cave the track rises very steeply. Walkers are faced with a further two hours of will and energy-sapping endeavour. At Johannes Notch, on the crater rim, there is a last heavy-legged scramble to Gillman's, and relative relief. Few people leap around in triumph, though the view which is revealed to them, as the sun climbs up beyond the turreted peaks of Mawenzi, far across The Saddle, usually gladdens the thumping heart. Even so, after a brief rest and group photographs, many people opt for those three much-recommended cures for altitude sickness – descent, descent, descent.

▲ *Above: Evening light on the exposed Barafu spur, one of the setting-off points for the final early-morning push to the summit.*

STRANGE THINGS AT THE TOP OF AFRICA

Animals, as well as flowers, have been seen at the top of Kilimanjaro, including the frozen carcass of a leopard, mentioned by Hemingway in *The Snows of Kilimanjaro*, and a small pack of wild dogs reported by that great explorer, Wilfred Thesiger. Odd things have gone on there too. Parachutists have landed on Kibo, hang-gliders have jumped off it, it has been climbed by a pair with their legs tied together, a party of blind people, an 85-year-old Spaniard (who vows he'll be back when he's 90), a motorcyclist has conquered it and a game of tiddlywinks has been played at the summit.

ARRANGEMENTS FOR CLIMBING KILIMANJARO

• Registered **guides** are obligatory, porters very much recommended.
• Most people climb Kilimanjaro via **package deals** through home-country travel agencies. Independent travellers will find operators in Arusha, Moshi or Marangu.
• A trek can cost from $2000–$5000 per person, depending on the company and the route. The fee includes camping, food, guides, park fees and transport to and from the mountain. It is probably best to spend at least $2400 per person.
• Cheaper climbs are available but not necessarily good value.
• Individuals can 'tailor' their own climbs but should allow extra time for this.
• Warm **clothing** and wind- and waterproof outers are essential (several light layers are better than a cumbersome one). Appropriate footwear, sleeping bag, sun protection and water bottles are among other necessities. Equipment can be hired in Marangu but climbers should not cut corners to save cash.

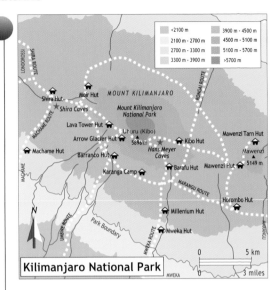

<2100 m		3900 m - 4500 m
2100 m - 2700 m		4500 m - 5100 m
2700 m - 3300 m		5100 m - 5700 m
3300 m - 3900 m		>5700 m

Kilimanjaro National Park

0   5 km
0   3 miles

But the experience will live with them forever. And the punishment and pain will all be forgotten. For to look down on Africa, from the top of Africa's highest mountain, is breathtaking metaphorically as well as literally. And the peak itself, with its wedding cake-like terraces of ice, and perhaps a fresh layer of snow in and around the symmetry of its remarkable crater, has a stark and sterile beauty of its own.

The true summit, **Uhuru Point**, is 210m (700ft) higher, and a further hour's struggle around the crater rim. For many Gillman's is enough, and almost everyone is glad when the time comes to go down. The descent over loosening scree should be treated with caution, but the long trek back from the base of Kibo to Mandara Hut is covered, by most people, surprisingly quickly (Horomobo Hut being bypassed).

◀ *Left: A high camp site on the Shira plateau.*
◀◀ *Opposite: On the roof of Africa. Smile and pretend you don't have a headache!*

Other Routes

Routes vary in difficulty, popularity and scenic beauty. The least difficult, most popular is **Marangu**, followed by **Rongai**; the more difficult routes are **Machame**, **Shira** and **Lemosho**. The longer routes such as Shira and Lemosho (crossing the Shira Plateau from the west) involve more hiking but better acclimatization. They also allow you to start your summit hike at less 'anti-social' hours!

The **Machame** route (from the southwest) is one of the more beautiful, as it ascends through the forest to emerge on the Shira Plateau, facing the magnificent Western Breach with its daunting Wall, though the route has become much more popular in recent years. The **Umbwe** and **Mweka** routes also pass through the forest, from the south, whilst in the west are the longer but more gradual routes across the Shira Plateau, the **Shira** and the **Lemosho**.

Vegetation

One of the many interesting effects of a five-kilometre-high free-standing mountain on the Equator is that it embraces a complete range of vegetational zones. On the lowest slopes, up to a height of about 1800m (5900ft), the land, of rich volcanic soil, is used for **pasture** and **cultivation**. The next zone is composed of **rainforest**. With an annual rainfall of over 2000mm (79in), it is lush, dense, and often girdled by mist. The rain and condensation

Kilimanjaro's famous giant lobelia hides some pretty flowers, which are visited by scarlet-tufted malachite sunbirds. The male is a metallic green bird with a long tail, its tiny scarlet tufts sometimes visible on either side of its chest. The smaller Eastern double-collared sun-bird is also found here. Other, less colourful birds to be seen on the moorland include augur and mountain buzzards, Shelley's francolins, Cape quail, Alpine swifts, stone chats, Hunter's cisticiolas and yellow-crowned canaries. Alpine chats, streaky seed-eaters and white-necked ravens might be seen around Horombo Hut. The chats are as tame and as perkily plump as European redbreasts. They might well be called the 'Kilimanjaro Robin' but they are true mountain birds, at home on the upland moors.

filters through the plants, humus, and porous volcanic rock. The water then runs underground along less porous strata of lava to emerge as springs on the lower slopes, where much of it is channelled into the sometimes ancient and ingenious irrigation schemes of the Chagga. Most of the wildlife found on the mountain occurs in the forest, including elephant, buffalo and leopard, but walkers are very unlikely to encounter them. More common are the black-and-white colobus monkey, or the blue-grey Sykes monkey, along with a number of birds.

From about 2800m (9200ft) to 4000m (13,100ft), the landscape becomes open **heath** and **moorland**. This is characterized by hardy heathers, some of which grow up to 9m (30ft) tall, and giant lobelias and senecios. *Lobelia deckenii*, the only giant lobelia found on Kilimanjaro, can sometimes grow up to 3m (10ft) in height. *Senecio kilimanjari* is one of two giant senecios found on the moors. It too is endemic, and grows as high as 5m (16ft). The senecios have thick shaggy stems, often branched, and are topped by great rosettes of leaves, like giant arti-chokes with open bracts. Like the lobelias they grow beside streams. Behind Horombo Huts, in the damp little valley below Mawenzi, a whole colony of them stand like monsters from another world.

▶ *Right: A rare, giant* Senecio kilimanjari *on the moorland zone.*

Above this, from 4000m (13,100ft), is the **'Alpine'** **desert**. It seems very bleak, ranging from freezing temperatures at night to blistering sunlight at midday. This constant freezing and thawing (called solifluction), loosens the soil, discouraging the growth of roots, but lichens are common, while one plant, a moss ball, rolls around feeding on the soil it picks up and the moisture it absorbs.

Little lives above 5000m (16,400ft), and though the **glaciers** of the summit are slowly reducing in size, much of the ground is constantly under ice and snow. One everlasting flower, *Helichrysum newii*, has learned to live in Kibo Crater, sustained by the heated soil alongside a fumarole. It is said to be the highest flower on earth.

ARUSHA

Arusha, 70km (45 miles) to the west of Moshi, is a livelier town than its neighbour. Situated beneath Mount Meru, it is base camp for most safaris in Tanzania's famous northern game reserves. Like many African towns, it has a half-neglected air, but tourism is bringing in money, hope and rising standards. A decent range of hotels, restaurants and curio shops are now springing up, and Arusha could well develop into the Nairobi of northern Tanzania.

CLIMBING MOUNT MERU

Guided climbs to the 4566m (14,990ft) high summit of Meru can be arranged through the park authorities or various safari companies. It is a three-day (two up, one down) trip. It is a pleasant climb, without the crowds or the more severe altitude problems associated with Kilimanjaro. Costs are lower as well, although you will need a registered guide, and good equipment is necessary on the upper slopes. The most common itinerary is to walk from Momela Gate to Miriakamba Hut on the first day, which allows a chance to explore the fantastic crater and ash cone. Day two is only a three-hour climb to Saddle Hut, at 3600m (11,800ft), from where the summit (4566m; 14,950ft) is four to five hours away, and normally attempted early the next morning. Coming down to Momela Gate takes about eight to nine hours. The best time to climb Meru is between October and February. Scenery, at whatever time of year, can be splendid.

◀ *Left: Arusha, the unassuming hub of Tanzania's beautiful and fascinating northern safari circuit.*

▲ Above: Mount Meru, the 'Black Mountain' to the Maasai, towers above the town of Arusha.

NGURDOTO CRATER

One of Arusha Park's prime attractions is Ngurdoto Crater. No human incursions on to the crater floor are permitted, and visitors must drive to the crater rim to look down into its entrancing green arena. It is 3km (2 miles) in diameter, and its forests and swamps are home to elephant, buffalo and other creatures. Red duiker might be observed in the forest during the steep ascent, and colobus monkeys, those handsome acrobats of the high canopy, are often to be seen close to one of the viewpoints on the crater rim.

Mount Meru ★★

Like Kilimanjaro, Mount Meru is volcanic, but its dark peaks and ridges are more mountain-like than the Christmas pudding Kilimanjaro, its collapsed crater floor tucked away amid the forest, far below the summit. This crater is a most impressive place, silent, almost eerie, half-encircled by a ghostly forest of lichen-hung trees. A precipitous ash cone rises from it, backed by its own darkly forbidding wall, over 1500m (4900ft) high. Meru is part of Arusha National Park, and it is possible to walk to the crater through the rainforest, from the park's Momela Gate. The ascent is straightforward and takes about three or four hours (see panel on page 55 for details of climb).

There are elephant and buffalo on Meru, and the possibility of strolling around a corner to find several tonnes of muscle and bone twitching, stamping and snorting demands that you are accompanied by an armed ranger. The actual danger is minimal, but there might be times when this is hard to believe. Less threatening creatures live here too, among them the shy and handsome bushbuck. Sensitive walkers, if they stay silent and still, might get good views of these.

Arusha National Park ★★

The park which Meru overlooks is overlooked in a different sense by many tourists, who rush by to more spectacular places, yet Arusha National Park is among the most beautiful in Africa. With Meru in its western corridor, and Kilimanjaro to the east, it encompasses placid alkaline lakes, montane forest and open glades. Once only 137km² (53 sq miles) in area, it now covers 552km² (213 sq miles). Its rhino have been obliterated and its elephant, harassed by poachers, have largely taken to the hills, but Arusha retains a superb range of flora and fauna. Other mammals in the park include leopard, hyena, baboon, hippo, zebra, giraffe, waterbuck, dik-dik and warthog. Bird life is prolific, especially around the **Momella Lakes**.

THE FRINGES OF THE MAASAI STEPPE
Tarangire National Park ★★

A very different, but even more exciting, national park is Tarangire, across the Ardai Plains west of Arusha. Named after the shallow but important river which passes through it, Tarangire is 'on' when the southern Serengeti is 'off', with huge numbers of game sustained by the river throughout the dry season (roughly from July–October).

Tarangire is one of the few places in Africa where elephants can sometimes be seen in herds of 300 or more, and lion are quite common, especially during the dry season when huge numbers of wildebeest and zebra trek in from the Steppe tired and unwary. Black rhino were once common, but were almost all exterminated in the 1980s. There is also an impressive number and diversity of birds, while the country itself, particularly in the northern areas with their umbrella thorns and elephant-battered boababs, is quintessential 'real Africa'.

▼ *Below: The Tarangire River provides welcome relief in an otherwise dessicated dry-season landscape.*

▶ *Right: Elephants, the living barometers of successful management in many game parks, on the move in Mkomazi.*

Mkomazi National Park *

Across the Maasai Steppe, 125km (78 miles) or so south of Moshi, is another game sanctuary, Mkomazi. Access is via **Same** (rhymes with 'army') township through a gap in the Pare Mountains.

From these lovely ranges German guns once bombarded the British-led forces as they chased their elusive enemies south along the adjacent railway line during World War I. Same is peaceful now, and the Pare people characteristically gentle and obliging. But those one-time warriors, the Maasai, were roused to fighting mood again (in the courts rather than with spears) when evicted from the area in recent years. Peace seems to have prevailed and Mkomazi, a full national park now rather than a game reserve, is beginning to attract the attention of the safari companies and their clients. There is a camp inside the park and several small hotels and guesthouses in nearby Same.

Mkomazi's game is still quite wild despite decades of poaching and hunting, and although visitors might not see as much, in terms of numbers, as they will in the better-known sanctuaries, the park is as pretty a piece of bush as you are likely to see in Africa and any animals are a bonus. Possibilities include lion, leopard, cheetah, elephant, buffalo, eland, fringe-eared oryx, hartebeest, zebra, giraffe, Grant's gazelle and the shy aardwolf. The endangered black rhino and wild dog are both being bred, for eventual release in the wild, in the park. Birding is excellent.

Lushoto *

South of Same and the Pares are the **Western Usambaras**, another lovely range of mountains. A pleasant 110km (70-mile) drive from Mkomazi, with the mountains to the east and the Maasai plains to the west, brings the traveller to **Mombo**. From here a good road winds up into the Usambaras to Lushoto, 25km (15 miles) away. The drive alone is worth the diversion, for the scenery, especially in good light, is extremely picturesque.

Lushoto, sited on the slopes and terraces of a pleasant upland valley, was obviously popular with the colonial Germans, who, acknowledging its situation and relatively mild climate, thought of making it their capital. Even now the administrative buildings, missions and churches around the town proclaim their European derivation. The vicinity of Lushoto is very fertile, producing vegetables and fruits for the markets of Dar and elsewhere.

WALKING IN THE USAMBARAS

There are some fine walking tracks around Lushoto, many of them gently graded paths leading through the montane forest or up the hillsides. Although widely cultivated, the Western Usambaras offer some magnificent scenery, and the forests protect a spectacular number of endemic plants. One of the most rewarding walks is to a place called The Viewpoint, a comfortable one-hour hike from Lushoto, via Irente. The views from this vantage point, across the course of the Pangani and the Maasai Steppe beyond, are very impressive. Ask at the hotels for other recommendations.

▼ Below: The expanse of the Maasai Steppe and the small town of Mombo.

BEST TIMES TO VISIT

The north is generally pleasant all year, though the rains (mid-March to May and mid-October to mid-December) can be inconvenient. The period from mid-May to mid-October is noticeably drier and cooler.

GETTING THERE

A few **international airlines** fly into Kilimanjaro Airport, between Moshi and Arusha, including KLM, Air France, Lufthansa, Kenyan Airways and Ethiopian Airlines. An alternative is to take onward **charter** flights or long-distance buses from Kenya or Dar.

GETTING AROUND

Most visitors travel on **pre-arranged package tours**. For independent travellers there are many safari companies in Arusha and Moshi. **Taxis** are available in Moshi and Arusha and there are **car hire** firms in each town, including some of the travel companies. A good **shuttle-bus** service (Riverside) connects Moshi, Arusha and Nairobi (Kenya) twice daily.

WHERE TO STAY

Listed Marangu/Moshi hotels organize Kilimanjaro climbs.

Marangu

Marangu Hotel, tel: 027 275 6594, info@maranguhotel. com www.maranguhotel.com Popular. Pleasant gardens.

Kibo Hotel, tel: 027 275 1308. German period, recently renovated but still oozes character.

Moshi

AMEG Lodge, tel: 075 405 8268, info@ameglodge.com www.ameglodge.com Probably best in-town option.

Mountain Inn, tel: 027 275 2370, info@kilimanjaro-shah. com www.kilimanjaro-shah. com 6km east of Moshi, unpretentious, good value. Pool, climbs of Kilimanjaro/Meru.

Crane Hotel, tel: 027 275 1114, reservations@kiliman jarocranehotels.com www. kilimanjarocranehotels.com One of best hotels in Moshi town centre.

Arusha Area

Unless on business or keen to stay in town, hotels outside central Arusha are perhaps preferable.

Town Centre

Mount Meru Hotel, tel: 027 254 5111, info@mountmeru hotel.com www.mountmeru hotel.com Large hotel, main Arusha-Nairobi road.

African Tulip, tel: 027 254 3004/5, info@theafricantulip. com www.theafricantulip.com Luxury boutique hotel. Good reputation, particularly suited to business travellers.

Kibo Palace, tel: 027 254 4472, info@kibopalacehotel. com www.kibopalacehotel. com Another good hotel if you want to be in town.

East of Town

Arumeru River Lodge, tel: 073 297 9908, info@arumeru lodge.com www.arumeru lodge.com Well-run luxury lodge 20km east of Arusha.

Rivertrees Country Inn, tel: 073 297 1667, info@rivertrees. com www.rivertrees.com Attractively restored farmhouse by Arusha/Moshi road, 20km east of Arusha. Up-market but reasonably priced.

Ngare Sero Mountain Lodge, tel: 073 297 8931, NgareSero @gmail.com www.ngare-sero-lodge.com Long popular with expats, now extended but retaining much of its original charm. Located 20km east of Arusha.

Hatari Lodge, tel: 075 255 3456, marlies@theafrican embassy.com Beautiful location by much-underrated Arusha National Park.

Kikongoni Lodge, tel: 027 255 3087, manager@kikongoni. net www.kikongoni.net 10km east of Arusha. Relatively up-market, excellent reviews.

Moivaro Coffee Lodge, tel: 027 250 6315/86, www.moivaro.com Mid-range lodge, 7 km. east of Arusha. Very good reputation.

Arusha Safari Lodge, contact details as for Moivaro (above), to which this lodge is a more up-market, well-recommended annexe, 10km east of Arusha.

Onsea House, tel: 078 711 2498, info@onseahouse.com www.onseahouse.com This is a luxury boutique hotel, located in a semi-rural setting 7km east of Arusha.

Dik-Dik, tel: 027 255 3499, dikdik@habari.co.tz www. dikdik.ch Another old favourite with expats. Organizes climbs of Kilimanjaro.

West of Town

Arusha Coffee Lodge, tel: 027 250 0630/9, videar@elewana.com www.elewanacollection.com Well-reviewed luxury lodge on working coffee farm, western edge of town.

Tarangire National Park

Inside park:

Oliver's Camp, tel: 027 250 4118, reservations@asiliaafrica.com www.asiliaafrica.com Small camp in one of Tarangire's less-visited areas. Not cheap but excellent.

Swala Camp, tel: 0207 190 7728, info@sanctuaryretreats.com www.sanctuaryretreats.com Another excellent luxury camp, though it is fairly remote by road. Located in west-central Tarangire.

Tarangire Safari Lodge, tel: 027 254 4752, bookings@tarangiresafarilodge.com www.tarangiresafarilodge.com This lodge has the best location in park, though the area is much busier than formerly. Unpretentious, this relatively inexpensive lodge has long been popular with 'old Africa hands'.

Outside park:

There are quite a few camps outside Tarangire, mostly quite good, though getting in and out of the park is definitely a drawback, which is why they are not featured here.

Mkomazi National Park

Babu's Camp, tel: 027 254 8840, inquiries@babuscamp.com www.babuscamp.com Quite good, but confirm your reservations beforehand if wishing to visit rhino breeding project.

Lushoto

No outstanding options; among better ones are:

Eddie's Lodge, tel: 078 436 0624, lushotoexecutivelodge@bol.co.tz www.eddieslodge.com Simple, quite pleasant.

Lawns Hotel, tel: 078 442 0252, enquiries@lawnshotel.com www.lawnshotel.com It's showing its age (100 years old) but it has character, and an engaging managing director (Tony).

WHERE TO EAT

There are no outstanding options (outside good hotels) in Moshi/Arusha, but better ones include:

Moshi

Tanzania Coffee Lounge (good, popular café), **Deli Chez** (Indian veg/non-veg and continental), **Chrisburgers** (fast food), **Coffee Shop** (cakes, pastries, pizzas, etc.), **Indotaliano Restaurant** (good Indian/Italian cuisine), **Panda Chinese** and **El Rancho** (Indian).

Arusha

Bamboo Café (continental, Indian, Tanzanian), **Mc Moody's** (burgers, etc.), **Pepe's** (good Italian), **Shanghai**, **Pete's Place** (barbecue), **Impala Hotel** (Italian, Chinese, Continental), **Big Bite** (Indian, pricey but good), **Dragon Pearl** (Chinese) and **Bay Leaf** (pricey but good continental).

TOURS AND EXCURSIONS

Arusha National Park (superb scenery, wildlife), various **cultural tours** (ask your hotel/tour operator), **camel safaris** (www.mkurucamelsafari.com), **Ndarakwai Ranch Camp**, near Moshi (www.ndarakwai.com).

USEFUL CONTACTS

Arusha/Moshi Code: 027 **Arusha airport**, tel: 027 250 5980; **Kilimanjaro Airport**, tel: 027 255 4252.
Mt Meru Hospital, tel: (Arusha) 027 250 3352; **KCMC Hospital**, tel: (Moshi) 027 275 4377; **AAR Arusha Medical Centre**, tel: 027 250 1593; **AICC Hospital**, tel: 027 254 4113; **Flying Doctor**, tel: 027 250 2830.
TANAPA (Tanzanian National Parks:
www.tanzaniaparks.com

KILIMANJARO	J	F	M	A	M	J	J	A	S	O	N	D
AVERAGE TEMP. °F	77	79	77	75	73	70	70	70	72	75	77	77
AVERAGE TEMP. °C	25	26	25	24	23	21	21	21	22	24	25	25
RAINFALL in	2	2	5	12	6	1	1	1	1	1	2	2
RAINFALL mm	39	44	117	303	157	31	14	14	15	33	55	48
DAYS OF RAINFALL	4	4	8	17	14	5	3	3	3	4	6	6

4
Ngorongoro and the Serengeti

Close to Tarangire, on the Arusha-Dodoma road, is the settlement of **Makuyuni** (Place of the Fig Tree). It is small and unprepossessing but it has significance. For the road which leads from it, across the **Rift Valley**, takes travellers through a sector of **Maasailand**, past **Lake Manyara** and its adjoining national park, up the steep western wall of the Rift and across the rolling, fertile **Mbulu Plateau**. Beyond rises **Ngorongoro**, encompassing its famous crater. And beyond Ngorongoro the track descends to the **Serengeti** plains through some of Africa's most superb scenery.

The world famous short-grass plains can be dusty and disappointingly 'empty' in the dry season. But from around mid-December to the beginning of June, with the grass green and the great migration making the most of it, the experience can be awesome. Great congregations of wildebeeste and zebra, soft-focused in the mists beneath Lemagrut, or flooding the plains between Naabi Hill and Ndutu, stagger the mind and senses.

THE RIFT VALLEY

The track which crosses the Rift from Makuyuni to Mto Wa Mbu (an interesting and enterprising town beneath the Rift's western wall) has recently been upgraded and tarred. Old Africa hands will wonder what the world is coming to, as the old track was straight out of Hell. As was, in a way, the Rift itself...which was formed as continental drift tore East Africa apart, dropping in a series of

◀ *Opposite: Migrating wilde-beest take the plunge at the Mara River.*

DON'T MISS

*** Ngorongoro Crater: world famous 'bowl' of wildlife. Best place to see rhino in Tanzania.
*** Serengeti migration: best in December and January, when the herds are in the southern plains and the weather is usually favourable (but *see* panel on page 74).
** Lake Manyara National Park: fine setting, with elephants, tree-climbing lions and flamingoes.
* Olduvai Gorge: site of Louis and Mary Leakey's famous archeological finds.

▶ *Opposite: Once much feared, now much photographed – the proud and colourful warriors of Maasailand.*

blocks along parallel fault lines, resulting eventually in a system of irregular valleys, which stretches from the Dead Sea to Mozambique.

Parts of the Rift Valley, especially by Ol Doinyo Lengai ('Mountain of God' to the Maasai), have a hard, spare beauty, founded on geological violence. Lengai itself remains violent – it rises, just outside the north-eastern corner of the Ngorongoro Conservation Unit in a steep cone to 2768m (9082ft). In 1966 it blew its main vent, spewing a plume of gas and cinders 1500m (5000ft) into the air, coating the mountain and the downwind plains with caustic ash. It overlooks the bitter, alkaline waters of **Lake Natron**, a breeding ground of the lesser flamingo.

The Maasai

The Rift is Maasai country. Tourists travelling down the road to Mto-Wa-Mbu, under the western Rift wall, will see the Maasai and their God-given cattle, as well as *enkang*, the circular arrangements of huts where the families and their cattle live. *Murran* (more commonly *moran*), the young warriors, live in their own *manyattas* elsewhere, with some of the *ndito* – the unmarried girls.

The Maasai have been much admired and romanticized. They are a fascinating people, many of whom cling to a traditional lifestyle. The men wear red blankets draped over their shoulders, carry spears or sticks and cover their hair and bodies with sheepfat and ochre. Livestock are central to their lives, and their diet still includes cow's blood

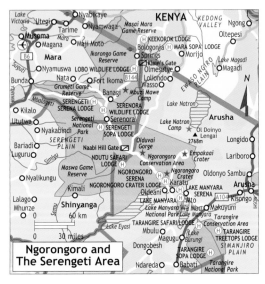

Ngorongoro and The Serengeti Area

mixed with milk. They appear to be at one with their environment, but life is still harsh: traditionally children often have two lower incisors knocked out to allow feeding in the event of lockjaw, and male and female circumcision is still carried out without anaesthetic (*see panel, page 25*). Maasai are not, however, unaffected by tourism, and tourists wanting to photograph them can expect to haggle for the privilege.

Lake Manyara National Park **

Mto Wa Mbu (Mosquito River) is well named, and well situated. The little settlement has become a popular stop-over for tourists and campers, providing them with souvenirs, fuel and basic groceries. Its population is ethnically mixed. Just beyond the township, to the south, is Lake Manyara National Park, between the lake and the Rift wall.

This 330km² (127-sq-mile) park is known for its **elephants** and its **tree-climbing lions,** as well as the **flamingoes** and other fascinating **birds** which can be seen in impressive numbers on and around the shallow, alkaline lake. The area was once famous among big game hunters (one of them, Ernest Hemingway, describes it in *The Green Hills of Africa*). The elephant suffered drastically from the

MAASAI HUTS

Travellers across the Rift will see the circular *enkang* or family settlements of the Maasai, sometimes surrounded by a barrier of euphorbia or thorn trees, which keep cattle in and leopards and lions out. The low, loaf-shaped huts, built by the women from saplings and waterproof coverings of cow dung are traditionally divided, by a screen, into two rooms, with a convoluted entrance hall between. Calves or goats are sometimes housed in this hallway at night. The main herds spend the night in the centre of the *enkang*, surrounded by their own little stockade. Each hut in an *enkang* has a special place, according to the status of its occupants.

65

THE LERAI FOREST

One of the most noticeable features of Ngorongoro Crater, when seen from the rim, is the Lerai Forest. Its name derives from the Maasai word for the yellow-bark acacia trees, which were once called 'fever trees' – a matter of guilt by association, for they grow in damp habitats, often alongside standing water, which of course is a wonderful breeding ground for the anopheles mosquito. The Lerai sometimes harbours bull elephant and waterbuck, but less than 30 years ago 23 rhino were resident in the forest, an amazing density of 7 rhino to the square kilometre (19 to the square mile). Other major features of the Crater include Lake Makat (the name means 'soda' in Maasai), the Mandusi and Gorigor swamps, and Engitate Hill.

highly organized poaching of the 1980s, but are now recovering. Other big game, including lion, is often seen, despite the fairly dense forest and bush. There are stretches of more open country by the lake.

Visitors often rush through Manyara's gloomy **ground-water forest,** the lovely *acacia tortilis* **woodland** and along the **soda flats** of its lake, before driving on to lunch at Ngorongoro. Yet Manyara has much to offer to those who can afford to stay for a day or more; one geologically interesting attraction are the **hot springs** at the far end of the park.

NGORONGORO CRATER

From Manyara the road makes a steep ascent up the Rift Wall (don't miss the fine views from the little lay-by near the top). The track then crosses the rolling **Mbulu Plateau**, rich farming country tilled by the Mbulu people (more properly the Iraqw). Beyond this lies the steep, thickly forested side of the Ngorongoro Crater, arguably the most famous wildlife refuge in the world. From the lodges on the crater rim, at about 2400m (8000ft), you look down upon the near-circular crater floor, an expanse of flat, open grassland, forest and lake 14km (9 miles) across. Around it stands a ring of extinct volcanoes with poetic Maasai names, and within the beautiful irregularity of the

◀ *Left: Lake Makat (a Maasai word meaning 'soda') on the floor of Ngorongoro Crater.*
◀◀ *Opposite: A chance to relax by the swimming pool of Lake Manyara Hotel, over-looking the Rift Valley.*

bowl, something like 20,000 large or moderately large animals live out their lives. The crater (more accurately caldera) is a remarkable natural amphitheatre which properly takes its place as one of the essential highlights of East Africa.

The crater once belonged to the Maasai. In 1958 they signed away their right to live there, though they still take their cattle down to the soda-licks around Lake Makat. Sometimes they can be seen, striding across their old pastures with their herds, raising the dust of history as well as the volcanic soil. Red shukas streaming in the breeze, spears gleaming in the sun, they make a fine and moving sight.

Earlier in the 20th century the crater was occupied by German (and later British) farmers and squatters. In 1954 the squatters were evicted, and in 1959 the Conservation Area was inaugurated.

Visitors to Ngorongoro commonly arrive at one of the lodges after a day's trip from Arusha and Lake Manyara. The next morning they descend into the crater, 600m (2000ft) below, a volcanic basin where, despite the prevailing atmosphere of tranquillity, an abundance of animals jostle for a place in an intricately poised struggle for survival. In many ways the crater provides its tenants

FARMERS IN EDEN

In the early years of the 20th century two German brothers, **Friedrich and Adolph Siedentopf**, farmed the fabulous Ngorongoro Crater. The ruins of both farms can still be seen, one behind the Lerai Forest and the other across the crater on the slopes above the Munge Stream. They and their cattle shared the land with the **Maasai**, and of course some pretty eclectic farm animals, such as rhino and elephant. The Maasai, who believe that they own all the cattle in the world, sometimes 'claimed back' a few German beasts, and lion, which were often shot on sight as vermin, took a few more. The outbreak of World War I forced the brothers to leave Ngorongoro.

RHINO ROMEOS AND OTHER STRANGE AFFAIRS

- **Rhino** numbers are at endangered levels, but when boy *does* meet girl, they make the most of it – copulation can last up to an hour.
- Moral and genetic problems over incestuous relationships in the confines of the Crater do not trouble the **lions**, as mating seems to be one of their main preoccupations. Lionesses need repetitive sexual stimulation before they ovulate, which keeps the handsome and often black-maned lions of Ngorongoro fairly busy.
- Female **hyenas** have taken feminism to fascinating extremes – they are larger and more dominant than males, and are equipped with identical sexual organs (in terms of size and shape, even when erect). Although they are not hermaphrodite, the male hyena, when his fancy turns to thoughts of love, is confronted by a partner exactly like himself but bigger, which cannot be all that good for the ego.

with their every need, but the rent in paradise can be very high, and is often paid in blood. Ngorongoro is not the open zoo that it sometimes seems to be; the animals are wild, and it is important to remember this.

The Wildlife

The number of **lion** on the crater floor varies, but is often around 100. Because of the nature of the crater, and the abundance of food, there is little pressure on the lions to move out, and much resistance to lions trying to move in. Consequently, many of Ngorongoro's lions are said to be closely related, which might (or might not) prove genetically damaging.

Lion are always popular, but the animal most tourists hope to to see in the crater is the **black rhino**, as Ngorongoro is one of the few places left in Africa where this much-persecuted creature can be seen in the wild. In the mid-1960s the biologist John Goddard recorded 110 rhinos on the crater floor. These were reduced to about 10 or 12 by the poaching epidemic of the 1980s. Since then, numbers in the crater have increased to about 20, thanks to more effective protection, though repopulation is slow, with gestation alone averaging 15 months.

▶▶ *Opposite: A vehicle negotiates the steep and winding ascent road out of Ngorongoro Crater.*
▶ *Right: A bull elephant reminds safari companies that he has right of way in Ngorongoro Crater.*

Another much-maligned animal in Ngorongoro is the **spotted hyena**. Like lion, hyena are largely active at night, and are great opportunists. Contrary to former opinion, however, they are very efficient hunters, and in Ngorongoro the image of the cowardly, skulking scavenger has been finally laid to rest. There are about eight clans living in Ngorongoro in their respective territories across the crater floor, each clan composed of 10 to 100 members. They are capable of keeping up a near-tireless, loping run, and of bringing down prey as large as adult wildebeest and zebra. Hyena kill about one quarter of all the new-born wildebeest in the crater each year, and are responsible for more overall kills than the lions, which, ironically, scavenge from the hyena.

Ngorongoro teems with other interesting species and in the crater there is rarely a dull moment. There seem to be animals everywhere – **elephant**, **wildebeest**, **zebra**, **buffalo**, **eland**, **Grant's** and **Thomson's gazelle**, **warthog** and many others, including the leggy and attractively spotted **serval cat** which patrols the taller grasslands, pouncing on mice or leaping from cover to claw birds from the air. The crater floor is perfect for **larks, long-claws**, **pipits** and **plovers**, as it is for the much larger **ostriches**, **Kori bustards** and the elegant **crowned cranes**.

NOT JUST THE CRATER

The Crater is only a small part of the Ngorongoro Conservation Area, 8300km^2 (3200 sq miles) in extent, and a unique experiment in multiple land use. Its main features are the Crater Highlands (of which the famous crater is a small part) and the short-grass plains beyond, which merge with the vast grasslands of the adjacent Serengeti National Park.

Wildlife is protected throughout the area, with elephant, buffalo, leopard, bushbuck and a host of other animals being present, sometimes surprisingly close to the lodges on the crater's edge. Birds are abundant along the forested rim, and in and around the lodge gardens.

▲ *Above: Olduvai Gorge, site of many exciting discoveries.*
▶ *Opposite: A balloon drifts silently over the Serengeti.*

Olduvai Gorge *

Ngorongoro Crater has its share of archeological sites, and at least one splendid and sacred fig tree, said to have grown from the grave of a Barabaig warrior chief. But the track which passes between the crater rim and the slopes of Oldeani, the 'Mountain of Bamboo', then curves down towards the Serengeti, eventually crossing a slight but famous rocky gorge, where history has literally been laid bare.

In 1931 **Dr Louis Leakey**, following up previous explorations of Olduvai by a German professor, found human remains here. In 1959, after almost three decades of unrelenting work, Louis' wife **Mary** came running back to camp crying 'I've got him! I've got him!' The gentleman in question was nearly 2 million years old, and Mary had uncovered fragments of his skull. She named him 'Nutcracker Man' (*Australopithacus boisei*). Remains of 'Handy Man' (*Homo habilis*) – also about 1.8 million years old – were found later.

An even more exciting find came in 1976, when Mary Leakey discovered, in petrified volcanic ash at **Laetoli**, 20km (12 miles) south of Olduvai, the clearly preserved footprints of three hominids. One was relatively large – though no more than 1.4m (4ft 7in), one medium-sized, and one small: perhaps a man, woman and child, if such terms are appropriate for hominids with a brain less than a third the size of our own. Whatever they were, they walked upright, and their stroll was 3.5 million years ago.

There is a visitors' centre at Olduvai, with an interesting little museum and guided tours of the immediate gorge for those who choose to take them. Unless visitors are particularly interested, an hour in the vicinity is long enough.

SERENGETI NATIONAL PARK

Both Olduvai and Laetoli are on the edge of the Serengeti, 'The Great Open Place' to the Maasai. The Maasai lost the Serengeti, along with Ngorongoro, when the areas were made into National Parks, but at places such as the Gong Rock at **Moru Kopjes**, where the impact of a large rock being struck by smaller ones rings out across the great plains, there is evidence of the warriors' passing. Rangers will tell you that the *Il murran* would strike the rock to guide their cattle-raiding comrades home, but knowing the warriors, they probably did it just to amuse themselves. There is a cave on another nearby kopje, with Maasai rock-paintings (relatively recent) by its entrance, depicting shields and figures.

Kopjes – outcrops of granite rock – rise like shimmering islands in the Serengeti's sea of grass, and are a most attractive feature of the Park. One of them, **Naabi Hill,** marks the major gate of the Serengeti, commanding the most beautiful acacia and short-grass savanna, the plains sweeping away on every hand as if to challenge the concept of the horizon.

Big Cats

Much of the southern Serengeti is ideal cheetah habitat, especially by the Gol Kopjes, where there is firm, open space, often lots of Thomson's and Grant's

SERENGETI KOPJES

Kopje (pronounced 'copy') is a Dutch word meaning small hill. The Serengeti kopjes consist of old granite rock, broken and worn by constant expansion and contraction due to abrupt temperature changes. Like oceanic islands, they have their own range of vegetation and wildlife, and are often home to lizards, hyrax and those delightful antelopes, the dik-dik. Snakes such as the spitting cobra and puff adder are sometimes found there, as are klipspringer antelope, lion and leopard. Close to the Naabi Hill–Seronera track and about 10km (6 miles) to the southeast of Seronera are the Simba Kopjes, always worth a visit, as are the Maasai Kopjes near Seronera itself. The Moru Kopjes are some 30km (20 miles) south of Seronera, and a pleasant place to spend the day, and enjoy a picnic lunch, or even camp.

BLACK-MANED LIONS

Male lions in Ngorongoro and the Serengeti often have beautiful black manes, once much prized by hunters. As a leonine means of showing off, bushy black manes, like bushy black beards, have their advantages, but when hunting on open grassland, an approaching black haystack must look as obvious, to a wildebeest or zebra, as a London taxi. Which might explain why female lions everywhere do most of the hunting and why, especially in the Crater, most lion scavenge from hyena in any case.

gazelles (the cheetah's preferred prey) and suitable cover among the longer turfts of grass. The leggy supermodels of the cat world are in their element here.

Lions enjoy the Serengeti too, as one might expect in what for them must seem like the biggest super-market on earth, with no-one manning the tills. And that other charismatic and exquisite feline, the **leopard**, is common, though not always commonly seen. More noc-turnal and shy than lions and cheetahs, the leopard can sometimes be found along the Seronera Valley, in the centre of the Park, or along other water-courses, resting in the trees or among the kopjes. If you are lucky enough to see one, don't spoil your observations or photo op-portunities by sudden movements or noises.

The Serengeti Migration

For the resident lion and spotted hyena, however, life is largely feast or famine, as the convenience foods on which they rely so much, wildebeest and zebra, have a disconcerting habit of disappearing. However, what is

frustrating for the cats is pure theatre for tourists, and the Serengeti migra-tion can well claim to be the greatest wildlife show on Earth.

Involving huge numbers of animals in a spectacular landscape, the migration is, at its best, almost over-whelming in its visual and emotional impact. The sanctuary in which it takes place is an enormous 14,763km^2 (5700 sq miles) in area, as big as Northern Ireland. It is adjoined by the **Masai Mara** across the border, **Maswa Game Reserve** to the west, and

◄ *Left: Wildebeest hard at work mowing the Serengeti plains.*
◄◄ *Opposite: A female cheetah with four young mouths to feed, scans the Musiara Plains.*

the **Ngorongoro Conservation Area** to the southeast. Two smaller game reserves, Grumeti and Ikorongo, now developed for tourism, lie to the northwest. Even by African standards, this is game country on a vast scale.

The animals involved in the migration move because they need to eat. Two million or more herbivores need a great amount of grass, and in the long dry season, from May to November, the short-grass plains to the south and southeast of Seronera are dessicated (and in any case shorn as short as suburban lawns by two million sets of incisors). So at the end of May or in early June (the timing varies, depending on the rains) the greatest natural circus in the world gets on the road. Its performers move out in files which can be 40km (25 miles) long, and the short-grass plains are sometimes virtually emptied of migratory animals within three or four days. It is this brief and unpredictable exodus which is so often filmed and photographed by those who are lucky enough to be around at the time.

The herds are followed, at least for some of the way, by the more nomadic predators – certain lions, hyenas and jackals. The long journey also takes the migrant

- As many as 1,500,000 wildebeest and 200,000 zebra take part, augmented by throngs of semi-migratory Thomson's gazelle, eland, topi and hartebeest. There can be densities of 500 wildebeest per square kilometre.
- To add to the turmoil, the beginning of the trek, in May or June, coincides with the wildebeest rutting period.
- The herds are constantly under threat from a variety of predators, including 1500 lion, 4000 hyena, 500 cheetah, as well as leopard and (in the Grumeti River) giant crocodiles. Many hyena actually commute, for distances of up to 60km (40 miles) or more, from their home bases, to find prey.
- In length, the journey from the short-grass plains and back again is 800km (500 miles).

NGORONGORO AND THE SERENGETI

WHEN TO SEE THE MIGRATION

For many people the most convenient time to see the migration is December to March inclusive, when it is in the Ngorongoro/Serengeti short-grass plains. Its most spectacular (but variable) phase, however, usually occurs in late May to early June, when it leaves the plains for the Western Corridor, crossing the Grumeti River in June and passing through the Grumeti Reserves in July/August. The northern Serengeti can be good in July as the herds pass through, and again in September/October as they return south. Timings vary depending on the rains. There are mobile camps that track the migration, as well as permanent camps and lodges. Many are listed (by area) in the 'At a Glance' section on pages 77–79.

herds through the home ranges of prides of lion and packs of hyena, and across rivers, such as the **Grumeti** and the **Mara**, where monstrous crocodiles lie in wait, to fling themselves upon drinking animals or twist great chunks from the corpses of those that drown.

The hazardous journey takes the herds out into the **Western Corridor** of the Serengeti, then far beyond the Kenyan border, before returning to the southern plains. It is a triangular trek of about 800km (500 miles) which some wildebeest will complete many times before disease or predators catch up with them, a testimony to their toughness. Surprisingly, however, an adult wildebeest can be brought down by a lion, or even a single hyena, with scarcely a groan of protest, despite its size and its horns, although a female zebra will often successfully defend her young ones against similar attacks.

The **return** to the short-grass plains is timed to co-incide with the Short Rains in December, and with the short and synchronized calving season which usually begins in January. Sometimes they (or the Gods) get it wrong: if the rains come late, or not at all, up to 80% of the new calves die due to lack of food. When they get it right, the scenes on the short grass, with hundreds of thousands of animals scattered across a whole landscape, and the calves skipping, running and bleating with apparent *joie de vivre*, are almost as spectacular as the exodus in May or June. And, of course, the timing is more convenient for tourists.

The wildebeests' travelling companions include large numbers of their antelope cousins, the **topi** and the **hartebeest** (*kongoni*). Their hind legs, shorter than the fore, act like low gears, to give them maximum acceleration from a standing start, and once on the move they are soon in overdrive. They are among the fastest of herbivores and, despite their ungainly shape, quite attractive.

Smaller Animals

One of the Serengeti's more interesting residents is the **honey-badger** – loose-skinned, powerfully jawed and, when it is aroused, utterly fearless. Their silver-grey and black coloration is for warning, not for camouflage, and honey-badgers (sometimes called *ratels*) will attack animals as large as buffalo, biting the prey's groin and genital organs and leaving the animal to bleed to death. Tourists, however, need not walk around in body armour, although the honey-badger has been known to attack car tyres.

Other smaller mammals of the Serengeti include the **black** or **silver-backed jackal**, **golden jackal**, **bat-eared fox**, **genet** (often to be seen around Ndutu Lodge), six species of **mongoose** and the skunk-like **zorilla**. Altogether there are almost 100 species of mammal found in the Park, and nearly 500 **birds**. Ground-nesting birds are abundant in the short-grass plains, as are the storks, vultures, eagles, hawks and falcons which thrive on the prodigality of the grasslands.

Around the Park

The short-grass plains of the southeastern Serengeti phase into an intermediate zone by **Naabi Hill**, and into long-grass plains closer to **Seronera**, where a lodge, a research institute and a visitors' centre are situated.

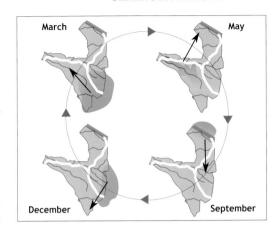

THE SERENGETI WILDEBEEST MIGRATION CYCLE

◀ *Opposite: A resting leopard lounges in the limbs of an acacia tree.*

DEFENDING WILDEBEEST

Wildebeest are not the clowns of the plains they are sometimes said to be. Nature hasn't blessed them with a high IQ but they are otherwise well adapted to a lifestyle which, in human terms, no insurance company would touch. A calf can stand almost as soon as it is born, and within an average time of seven minutes is able to run, albeit unsteadily, for its life. With a range of hungry predators on their tail, such precocity is very much in their interest. The wildebeest's lawnmower of a mouth is superbly designed to harvest grass – which is why they eat themselves out of house and home twice a year, and why they migrate.

▲ *Above: A klipspringer, the 'Goat of the Rocks', watches the world from a kopje.*

SWEET-TALKING BIRD

The myopic and misanthropic honey-badger has a remarkable relationship with the honey guide (the Latin name of which is – appropriately – *Indicator indicator*). The honey guide is a small bird which attracts the badger (and human honey-hunters) to wild bees' nests by its behaviour and calls. The badger then digs out the nest, and bird and mammal share the spoils. The bird gets the best of the deal – the honey-badger is, in fact, quite capable of finding its own hives.

About 18km (11 miles) north of Seronera is Banagi, and just to the east of here is **Kilimafedha**, the 'Hill of Wealth', so called because gold was mined here until 1966. The gold-bearing quartz is embedded in some of the most ancient rock on Earth, found between Banagi and Kilimafedha, and some two to three thousand million years old. The Serengeti is not short on superlatives.

Towards **Banagi**, and further northwards towards the Kenyan border, the country lifts into rolling uplands, fledged with bush and patchy woodland, relieved by open areas and ranges of hills. Many of the hills have crumbled into magnificent kopjes. The countryside in this vicinity is a joy to both the eye and the soul, and from August to November part of the great wildlife migration passes through, adding spectacle to splendour. Various lodges, as in other sectors of the park, are strategically situated in these areas (*see* At a Glance, pages 77–79).

Similarly well-placed lodges serve the **Western Corridor**, a tapering arm of the park which stretches to **Ndabaka Gate**, overlooking the shores of Lake Victoria. It is at its best, as far as game viewing is concerned, during the dry season from June to October. This is also the best time for travelling, as there are extensive black-cotton grasslands 30km (20 miles) east of Ndabaka. Black-cotton soil can be a nightmare during the rains, even for experienced off-the-road drivers in four-wheel-drive vehicles, and in the bush, discretion is almost always the better part of valour.

BEST TIMES TO VISIT

The long rains (mid-March to mid-May) and to a lesser extent the short rains (mid-October to mid-December) can cause certain tracks to become difficult or impassable but can be rewarding. Mid-May to mid-October generally dry and (late afternoon until mid-morning) pleasantly cool, even cold in the highlands.

GETTING THERE

Most visitors arrive by chartered aircraft, safari company vehicle or private car, via Arusha, which is the hub of the 'northern circuit'.

GETTING AROUND

Transport in and around the northern parks is almost entirely by safari company or private vehicles, operating out of or via Arusha. There is also a shuttle bus service connecting Arusha with Ngorongoro.

WHERE TO STAY

Lake Manyara Area
Manyara Tree Camp, tel: +27 11 809 4314, www.and beyondafrica.com Secluded, high-end camp towards southern extreme of park.
Lemala Manyara Camp, tel: 027 254 8966, res@lemala camp.com www.lemala camp.com Luxury tented camp by the lakeside, in the middle of the park.
Lake Manyara Serena, tel: 027 254 5555, lakemanyara @serena.co.tz www.serena

hotels.com This is probably the best of the options along the edge of the Rift wall. Fine views, just 15 minutes or so from park gates.
Lake Natron Camp, tel: 027 250 6315/86, www.moivaro. com Simple camp between an active volcano (Lengai – climbs are arranged) and the Rift Valley lake.

Ngorongoro Area
Crater Rim
Ngorongoro Crater Lodge, UK tel: +44 (0)20 7471 8780, USA tel: 1 866 356 469, www.ngorongoro-crater-lodge.com You either love this place for its over-the-top style or you hate it for the same reason. Whatever the case, it is a sumptuous place, superbly located, memorable and (perhaps also memorably) expensive.
Lemala Ngorongoro, tel: 027 254 8937, res@lemalacamp.com www.lemalacamp.com Very good luxury camp at northern end of crater, by Lemala descent road.
Ngorongoro Serena, tel: 027 254 5555, ngorongoro@serena.com www.serenahotels.com Pleasant lodge, cleverly concealed on inner lip of crater, not far from southern descent road. Mid-range (by Ngorongoro standards).
Ngorongoro Rhino Lodge, tel: 078 550 0005, rhino@ngorongoro.cc www.ngorongoro.cc Simple place set back from

the southern crater rim, and therefore by far the cheapest option in the area. Long-time favourite of less wealthy 'old Africa hands'/expats.

Karatu Area
Gibbs Farm, tel: 027 253 4397, reservations@gibbs farm.net www.gibbsfarm.net Old, much-loved coffee farm on the outer slopes of the Ngorongoro Crater, in Karatu. Advertised as a 'sanctuary for the senses', which it is.
Plantation Lodge, tel: 027 253 4364, info@plantation-lodge.com www.plantation-lodge.com High-end but homely lodge amid beautiful gardens, on the lower slopes of the outer crater rim. Swimming pool.

Ngorongoro Conservation Area/Southern Serengeti
Best December to March, when the migration is in the celebrated open grasslands. ('MC' after a name stands for 'Mobile Camp').

Olduvai Camp, tel: 078 422 8883, arusha@olduvai-camp.com www.olduvai camp.com A very special tented camp close to the famous Olduvai Gorge, Ngorongoro CA. The camp is hosted by Maasai.
Ndutu Safari Lodge, tel: 073 650 1045, info@ndutu.com www.ndutu.com Long-established, refreshingly independent, much-loved by 'old Africa hands' and expats, and by Serengeti standards

reasonably priced. Just on the Ngorongoro side of Ngorongoro/Serengeti boundary.

Lemala Ndutu (MC), tel: 027 254 8937, res@lemalacamp.com www.lemala.com Nine luxury tents on the edge of a marsh with lots of resident wildlife plus, in Dec–Mar, the migration.

Nomad Masek (MC), info@nomad-tanzania.com www.nomad-tanzania.com High-end mobile camp, only six tents and no obligatory sharing of vehicles.

Kusini Camp, UK tel: +44 (0)20 7190 7728, info @sanctuaryretreats.com www.sanctuaryretreats.com Twelve tented rooms in the extreme southwest of the Serengeti, between rocky outcrops and acacia woodland. Best times for the migration Jan–March.

Southeast Plains
Nomad Piaya, info@nomad-tanzania.com www.nomad-tanzania.com Up-market tented camp just outside the eastern boundary of the park, thus allowing foot safaris and night drives as well as regular game drives.

Sanjan Camp (MC), reservations@asiliaafrica.com www.asiliaafrica.com Sometimes called 'Suyan' Camp, this is another up-market tented camp located just outside the eastern boundary. The camps offers foot safaris and night (as well as daytime) game drives.

Gol Mountains Bivouac (MC), www.africatravelresource.com A simple, no-frills camp in a glorious, little-visited region. It is ideal for those who prefer a more authentic safari experience rather than luxury, and it's relatively inexpensive.

Central Serengeti
Resident game at all times, migration passing by to the west around May/June and to the east or through Seronera around November/December.

Dunia Camp, reservations@asiliaafrica.com www.asiliaafrica.com Much-recommended luxury tented camp among the attractive Moru Kopjes.

Serengeti Serena, tel: 027 254 5555, serengeti@serena.co.tz www.serena hotels.com Quite a large lodge catering largely for middle-range package tourists, but well-placed for game drives. Swimming pool.

Lemala Ewanjan (MC), tel: 027 254 8966, res@lemala camp.com www.lemala camp.com Genuinely luxurious tented camp based (except in April/May) in the renowned Seronera Valley.

Ronjo Bivouac (MC), UK tel: +44 (0)127 726 0280, tawisa.uk@talk21.com www.tanganyika.com This French-owned, Maasai-hosted light camp (dome tents) can be set up in central Serengeti any time of year. It is a refreshingly low-key, relatively low-cost alternative

to the up-market places. It's a real safari experience, so don't expect luxury.

Serengeti Western Corridor/ Grumeti Reserves
Migration crosses Grumeti around June and passes through Grumeti Reserves around July/August)

Nomad Mbalageti (MC), info@nomad-tanzania.com www.nomad-tanzania.com Small, high-end camp that operates in May/June when migration is in the Western Corridor. There is no obligatory sharing of vehicles.

Grumeti River Camp, SA tel (Johannesburg): +27 11 809 4300, www.andbeyondafrica.com This camps is pleasantly situated by an oxbow lake and close to the eerily portentous Grumeti River (*see* panel, page 79), home to giant crocodiles that prey on the migration as it crosses.

Mbalageti Lodge, tel: 028 262 2387, info@mbalageti. com www.mbalageti.com This is a fairly large lodge overlooking Mbalageti Plains. At its best during May/June, it is a mid-range alternative to the more up-market places.

Singita Grumeti, SA tel: +27 21 683 3424, enquiries@singita.com www.singita.com Singita Grumeti consists of three properties in an enormous private concession. It was recently voted 'best hotel in the world' for the second consecutive year. The migration passes through around May/June but there's resident game throughout year. Individual lodges/camps are:

Sasakwa Lodge – Luxury with a capital L. 'Grand colonial-style manor', splendid location.

Sabora Camp – the relatively modest annexe to Sasakwa. The accent is on 'relatively'. It is possibly the most luxurious camp in Tanzania.

Faru Faru – this is a high-end camp despite being the simplest of the three Singita options.

Serengeti North
The migration passes through this area around July and Sept/Oct.

Soit Sambu (MC), reservations@asiliaafrica.com www.asiliaafrica.com
This luxury tented camp is just outside the park boundary, so foot safaris and night drives are possible, as well as regular game drives.

Klein's Camp, SA tel: +27 11 809 4314, www.kleinscamp.com
A very good camp among hills just beyond the park boundary, so, as with Soit Sambu, foot safaris and night drives are possible, as well as regular game drives.

Lobo Lodge, tel: 027 254 8633, res@hotelsandlodges-tanzania.com www.hotels andlodges-tanzania.com
Former state property, now private. Rooms are uninspiring (but relatively low-cost),

and the lodge is imaginatively designed among granite outcrops overlooking a superb stretch of savannah.

WHERE TO EAT

Almost everyone eats in their lodges/camps, where the food is mostly good to excellent.

TOURS AND EXCURSIONS

Empakai Crater/Lengai: There are several popular guided hiking/camping treks in the Ngorongoro Conservation Area, to places such as Empakai Crater and the active volcano Ol Donyo Lengai, which trekkers can climb if they wish.

Olduvai Gorge: Another interesting diversion, just a short drive from Ngorongoro-Serengeti track. Historic site of Ancient Man; small museum.

Balloon Safaris: Operated from Seronera and other lodges. Champagne breakfast served on landing.

Cultural Tours: Available in and/or around Ngorongoro/Serengeti, including visits to Maasai, Datoga and Iraqw villages and Hadzabi hunter-gatherers. Ask your travel or safari company, or Contact the Arusha Travel Agency (*see* below).

GRUMETI RIVER

The main feature of the Western Corridor is the Grumeti River, which flows through the Corridor from east to west, and empties into Lake Victoria. Exceptionally large crocodiles live in this river, and visitors are advised not to stand or walk too close to the water's edge, for the huge reptiles are capable of surging from the river to grab unsuspecting wildebeest (or unsuspecting tourists). The less violent and extremely attractive colobus monkey lives in the canopy of the riverine forest, and that other magnificent black and white creature, the martial eagle, can sometimes be seen in the area.

USEFUL CONTACTS

Arusha/Moshi code: 027
Kilimanjaro Airport, tel: 027 255 4252.
AICC Hospital, tel: 027 254 4113.
Mt Meru Hospital, tel: (Arusha) 027 250 3352.
Flying Doctor, tel: 027 250 2830.
Arusha Travel Agency, tel: 075 598 9175, travel@arushatravelagency.com

NGORONGORO	J	F	M	A	M	J	J	A	S	O	N	D
AVERAGE TEMP. °F	70	70	70	70	66	63	63	64	66	68	70	70
AVERAGE TEMP. °C	21	21	21	21	19	17	17	18	19	20	21	21
RAINFALL in	3	3	5	10	3	1	0	0	0	1	4	4
RAINFALL mm	74	85	139	245	78	18	9	7	10	20	107	96
DAYS OF RAINFALL	9	9	13	21	13	4	3	2	2	2	10	11

5
The Lakes

It is difficult for most of us today to appreciate the fascination which the 'question of the Nile' held for the geographers, politicians and the better-informed general public of Victorian Britain. Explorers and missionaries tramped westwards from the east coast of Africa to the Lakes in search of the source of the sacred river and, perhaps, some kind of immortality. They mostly found mortality. Even Livingstone was brought to his knees, and an early death, in the swamps of Bangweulu (now in northern Zambia), hopelessly seduced by the search for those elusive headwaters. And the man who finally solved the nagging question, John Hanning Speke, shot himself soon afterwards and is now almost forgotten. Speke revealed that the Nile flows from the lake still called Victoria, though modern geographers have recently discovered a 'new' source northeast of Lake Tanganyika. Known by the Luo people of Kenya as *Nam Lolwe*, 'Lake Without End', Victoria is almost 70,000km² (27,000 sq miles) in area, the biggest lake in Africa and the second largest in the world.

Tanzania shares Lake Victoria with Kenya and Uganda, and **Lake Tanganyika**, 320km (200 miles) to the southwest, with Zaïre. Tanganyika, unlike Victoria, is a Rift Valley lake, and at more than 1433m (4700ft) is the second deepest in the world. It is also the world's longest freshwater lake. In the southwestern corner of the country is the third great lake, **Malawi**. Shared with both Malawi and Mozambique, it is another Rift Valley lake, overlooked by the magnificent Livingstone Mountains.

CLIMATE

The climate around the Lakes is very similar, in some respects, to that at the coast. The atmosphere can be oppressively hot and humid during the single rainy season, from the beginning of November to end of April, but generally the lakes themselves have a cooling effect, and temperatures are normally pleasant and constant. Minimum temperatures at Mwanza throughout the year are about 17°C (62°F) with maximums of 28°C (82°F).

◄ *Opposite: Canoes on Lake Tanganyika, a ready way to sell fresh produce.*

DON'T MISS

*** Rubondo Island National Park: tropical island seclusion, sitatunga, chimpanzees, lovely scenery and walks.
*** Mahale Mountains National Park: chimpanzees, remote seclusion, montane forest walks, birdlife, superb mountain scenery and sunsets across Lake Tanganyika.
*** Gombe Stream National Park: chimpanzees, site of well-known research by Dr Jane Goodall.
* Mwanza: restful little town on shores of Lake Victoria. Ferries to other parts of lake, including Bukoba in the west.
* Ujiji: site of H.M. Stanley's meeting with Livingstone.
* Lake Malawi: boat trips under Livingstone Mountains. Attractive scenery.

LAKE VICTORIA

John Speke first saw the lake he was to call Victoria on 3 August 1858, from a point where the town of **Mwanza** now stands. Speke was wondrously confident that he was looking at the lake which fed the Nile, and in memory of his momentous sighting the inlet he had been standing beside was later named Speke's Gulf.

The country through which he had marched from **Kazeh**, close to present-day **Tabora**, is largely unremarkable until the traveller approaches the lake, when the monotonous landscape is transformed into sweeping, almost treeless plains which are studded, like the Serengeti, with islands of granite. The air grows more humid and the land greener, for Victoria has its own micro-climate, and moods. Its shallow, normally placid waters tend to reflect the hues of the sky, and during storms its colour can almost match the blackness of its temper. On calm, fine days it glitters with a scintillating blueness, and its sunsets, from the eastern shores, can be astonishing in their reflected intensity. The writer Alan Moorehead has said that such scenes 'are very beautiful, and yet there is a mysterious and disturbing atmosphere about the lake. One feels here very strongly the primitiveness of Africa, its overwhelming multiplicity in emptiness.'

▼ *Below: The pleasant town of Mwanza, on the shores of Lake Victoria.*

Mwanza *

Mwanza, on Lake Victoria's southeastern corner, is a pleasant enough place, especially along its waterfront, where several tourist-class hotels are becoming established. For those who just want to relax, its air of unreproving indolence, broken only by the cries of the hadada ibis which roosts in the lakeside trees, can be a virtue in itself.

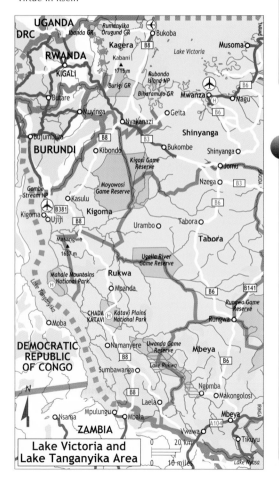

Lake Victoria and Lake Tanganyika Area

THE LAKES

THE AMPHIBIOUS SITATUNGA

The sitatunga resembles a long-legged bushbuck, but with fairly long, shaggy hair which is slightly oily, enabling them to spend much of their time in the water, or even completely immersed when threatened. Their splayed hooves allow them to step more easily across spongy mats of vegetation. On dry land, however, the hooves are something of a hindrance, making the animal more vulnerable to predators or hunters, though the sitatunga, like the bushbuck, will defend itself courageously against attackers, including men and dogs.

Mwanza's economy in recent years, apart from the fishing industry, has largely depended upon the agricultural produce of its fertile hinterland, farmed by the dominant tribe of the area, the **Sukuma**. The Sukuma are growers of cotton, maize and cassava, and they also herd cattle, although coffee shipped through the port originates in the West Lake Province, across the waters.

It is just a short ferry trip from Mwanza to **Saa Nane** (Two O'Clock) Island. Its small wildlife sanctuary badly needs upgrading but the island itself is quite attractive and worth a visit. Mwanza's best-known landmark, **Bismarck Rock**, can be seen from the nearby shore, to the west of the town.

Rubondo *

In the southwestern corner of Lake Victoria is a most delightful and unusual national park, Rubondo Island. Accessible by air (and sometimes by sea) from Mwanza, it is well worth the air charter prices or the longish boat journey. Its humid forest and wetland ecosystems are home to a number of indigenous species, such as the otherwise rarely encountered, semi-aquatic sitatunga, marsh mongooses and genet. There are also a few introduced animals, such as chimpanzees, roan antelope, giraffe and elephants. Plans to turn it into a sanctuary for black rhinos have so far been unsuccessful. It boasts an impressive variety of birds, some brilliantly varied butterflies, and among its array of beautiful plants are ground and tree orchids, fireball lilies which flower during the short rains, and the red coral tree which blossoms for most of the year. A simple but wonderfully situated little camp, ideal for honeymooners, occupies a clearing on the lakeshore, near the island's centre.

▼ Below: The prominent but precarious Bismarck Rock in Mwanza harbour.

◀ Left: Lake Victoria is an inland sea. Substantial ferries such as this one docked at Mwanza are used for inter-lake connections.

Bukoba *

The overlap between East and West Africa is a distinguishing characteristic of the West Lake Province, and a pleasant way of appreciating it is to sail from Mwanza to Bukoba, the western province's major town, on one of the Lake ferries. The Kagera region lies between the lake and Rwanda and Burundi, with Uganda to the north. It is considered, by some, to be the most attractive part of Tanzania.

Bukoba (founded by the ill-fated but brilliant eccentric, Emin Pasha) is situated on the lower slopes of the hills which overlook the lake. Rarely visited by tourists, it has an attractive location and restful atmosphere. Its hotels will never figure in the world's top ten but the best of them have a certain rural charm.

The people of Bukoba and of Kagera Region in general are **Haya**. Mostly Ugandan in origin, they are said to take quick advantage of formal education, though most of them are farmers, growing Robusta coffee, maize, beans, sweet potatoes and bananas. Like the Chagga, they have adopted the banana as their staple diet – they often eat them roasted, and served on banana leaves, accompanied by banana wine, which they sip through straws of grass.

Despite its remoteness, Bukoba has seen its share of action, defended by the Germans in World War I, and inaccurately bombed during Idi Amin's abortive incursions into Tanzania during the late 1970s.

BUKOBA'S WILDLIFE

Bukoba's westerly position is reflected in some of the bird species found there and in the adjacent region. Exciting species include:
• **Grey parrot:** the familiar talking parrot.
• **Ross's turaco**.
• **Eastern grey plantain eater:** which, of course, lives on bananas.
• **Northern brown-throated weaver:** often seen in the garden of the Lake Hotel.
• Anyone walking by the lakeside might be also be rewarded by the sight of **spotted-necked otters**, which will sometimes fish and frolic close to the shore in the clear blue waters of the lake.

THE LAKES

After two decades of determined exploring deep into Africa, David Livingstone was a well-known figure throughout the English-speaking world. Some deserters from his 1866 expedition past Lake Nyasa spread a rumour that he was dead, precipitating a search not resolved until Stanley, working for the *New York Times*, presumed to meet him under a mango tree in Ujiji. Stanley, who had dressed for the occasion and was very nervous (he half expected to be rebuffed), was later asked if he had actually uttered the famous phrase. 'Yes', he replied, 'I couldn't think what else to say.' The two got on well, explored regions of Lake Tanganyika together, and were said to have wept when they parted months later.

▼ *Below: The Mahale mountains, home of chimpanzees, rising from the shores of Lake Tanganyika.*

LAKE TANGANYIKA

Lake Tanganyika is one of the most interesting lakes in the world. The combination of antiquity (the dead 'fossil water' of its profound depths may be 20 million years old) and its isolation have produced many unique life forms. Most of the 250 species of fish which inhabit its rich upper waters are endemic, including many colourful cichlids, and a whole range of gastropods, molluscs and crustaceans. It even has a unique water snake, the Eastern aquatic cobra, which fishes by day and sleeps on the rocks by night. More aesthetically, Tanganyika often provides superb sunsets.

Ujiji *

If the waters of Tanganyika are filled with fascination, its shores are no less so. The topography to the east is largely monotonous, though **Henry Morton Stanley** 'regarded the alluring face of the land with a fatuous love'. Ujiji was the spot where Stanley finally caught up with **David Livingstone**, asking his famous question under a mango tree, which has now been replaced by a rather less attractive memorial. Ujiji's more general past, as an important terminus of the caravan route from the coast, is evident in the Arabic influences of Swahili-style houses, some with carved doors, and in a predominantly Muslim population. The town is quite large and spaciously laid out, and the shallow creek which passes for its harbour quite picturesque.

Kigoma *

Ujiji's importance declined with the ending of the slave and ivory trade, and it is now a satellite of Kigoma, 10km (6 miles) to the north. Kigoma came into prominence for the same reason as Ujiji – as the terminus of a trade route from the coast – although in Kigoma's case communications are by rail and the passengers leaving for the coast are not slaves. The **railway** was completed by the Germans in 1914, and soon afterwards appropriated by the British. For those who like to travel in style, it is not the best way to get to Kigoma, as the trip from Dar takes two days and is not the last word in comfort. But it beats walking all the way, as the explorers did.

Kigoma is a quiet town though its population and that of surrounding areas have been swollen by refugees from the Congo DR and Burundi. Its principle street slopes up from the interesting old station between mangoes and frangipani. Kigoma's main attraction is its lakeside location, and its role as a base for Mahale and Gombe chimpanzee sanctuaries.

Mahale Mountains National Park **

One of the destinations of the *Liemba* (*see* panel, this page) is **Magambo**, 115km (70 miles) south of Kigoma. A smaller boat then takes them to **Kasongo**, the headquarters of Mahale Mountains National Park. The complete trip from Kigoma takes about nine hours, and must be well planned and co-ordinated. Speedboats operate from the Hilltop Hotel in Kigoma, taking three to four hours, but are quite expensive. There are three luxury camps by the lake. There is a cheaper, self-catering option (Mango Tree Bandas) for anyone interested and willing to take on the challenge of getting there.

However, travellers should not be put off. Mahale Mountains is a delightful sanctuary, its lovely montane topography, draped in rainforest and inhabited by chimpanzees and other primates, with lower orders of animals, including birds and insects, being well represented.

Sunsets across the lake, and the fascinating lake itself, add to Mahale's isolated charms.

M. V. LIEMBA

Kigoma's most famous boat is an old lady with an interesting past: assembled from prefabricated sections at the start of World War I, she was fitted out with a 4.1 gun taken from the sunken battle-cruiser *Koenigsberg* and made ready for action. When the action came, however, the *Graf von Goetzen* (as she was then known) was sent to the bottom by a Belgian bomb. The British salvaged her in 1924, and after an extensive refit she was pressed back in service. She is still going strong, ferrying passengers to different parts of Lake Tanganyika.

Gombe Stream National Park ★★★

Gombe Stream, much closer to Kigoma and much smaller than Mahale, is similarly beautiful, though it has become isolated as surrounding forests have been destroyed. Only 25km (15 miles) north of Kigoma, it is accessible by boat. Water taxis operate from Kigoma, taking four to six hours. Speedboats take less than an hour.

Gombe is famous for its chimpanzees, though like Mahale it contains many other species of animals. The chimpanzees have been studied for decades, most famously by **Dr Jane Goodall**, who has been connected with Gombe since 1960. Sadly the Goodall Foundation is said to be less in evidence in Gombe than previously. The park has a mid-range lodge and a very basic rest house, where visitors need to be self-sufficient. Camping is possible by the shore.

Katavi Plains National Park ★

One of Tanzania's most remote and least-visited sanctuaries, Katavi is most easily accessed by air. By road (from Dar via Mbeya and Sumbawanga), the journey presently

◀ *Left: The flame of the Independence Monument adds warmth to the cool mountain air of Mbeya.*
◀◀ *Opposite: A chimpanzee, a primate found in both Mahale Mountains and Gombe Stream national parks on the shores of Lake Tanganyika.*

takes at least four days, so this is not a safari for the unadventurous. But the rewards are enormous, for Katavi's miombo woodland and long-grass plains are home to an impressive number of animals and birds. And the chances are that you'll have this chunk of 'real Africa' all to yourself. There are three small luxury camps, but independent campers need to be particularly self-sufficient.

THE SOUTHWEST
Mbeya *

Travellers to Mbeya, 900km (550 miles) southwest of Dar, will be tempted to stay. The town is small, and has little to offer tourists but relative peace and quiet but its location, among lovely mountain ranges, and its correspondingly cool climate, endear it to expatriates and travellers. There are a number of very pleasant walks in the hills, and a short drive away is Kitulo, Tanzania's smallest and newest national park, known locally as 'Bustari ya Mungu', the 'Garden of God'. From around Christmas until May the area, on the Kitulo Plateau, is a profusion of orchids and other flowers. Mbeya is also a good base from which to explore the lovely northern shores of Lake Malawi.

RELATIVES IN THE RAINFOREST

Remains of a hominid which lived four million years ago, recently discovered in Ethiopia, seem to confirm that our closest living relatives are the chimpanzees. Research at Gombe Stream, over rather fewer years, conforms to the same pattern. Chimpanzees have almost 100% compatibility with human DNA, a brain similar to that of man, and aspects of their behaviour are often compared to ours. Their relationships are close and complex, they hug, kiss and scream when excited or pleased, and become morbid or irritable when sad or thwarted. They sometimes use simple tools, hunt and kill monkeys, indulge in cannibalism and go to war, yet they remain fascinating and often loveable creatures.

Lake Malawi *

Malawi, smallest of the Great Lakes, is often known as Lake Nyasa in Tanzania, which claims part-ownership in a dispute with Malawi over natural gas fields beneath the lake bed. Despite the contentious politics and its distance from Tanzania's main tourist haunts, the lake is well worth the 130km (80-mile) detour (to the port of Itungi) by travellers who find themselves in Mbeya. Like Lake Tanganyika, Malawi is exceptionally rich in endemic species of fish and other aquatic creatures, and the scenery, with the Livingstone Mountains towering above the head of the lake, is quite splendid, especially when seen from a boat.

▲ Above: A fisherman's canoe beached on the shores of beautiful Lake Malawi.
▶ Right: Lake Malawi fishermen mending their nets by the shores of the great lake.

BEST TIMES TO VISIT

Rains (peaking Nov–Dec and Mar–Apr) can be dismal. Mid-May to mid-October is much drier and (in mornings and evenings) pleasantly cool.

GETTING THERE

Internal flights from Arusha or Dar the only reasonable options as road and rail journeys are long and gruelling.

GETTING AROUND

Taxis are available in main towns. There are a few travel companies in Mwanza and Kigoma. Internal flights operate to/from Mwanza and Kigoma and regular (though not state-of-the-art) ferries ply the lakes.

WHERE TO STAY

Lake Victoria
MWANZA

Malaika Beach Resort, tel: 028 256 1111/2222, info@malaika beachresort.com www.malaika beachresort.com Pleasant mid-range lakeside hotel.
Nyumbani Hotel, tel: 028 250 5021–3, info@nyumbani hotels.com www.nyumbani hotels.com Reasonable new hotel, town centre.
Tilapia Hotel, tel: 028 250 0517/617, info@hoteltilapia. com www.tilapiahotel.com Old lakeside favourite, recently upgraded. Four restaurants, swimming pool, free internet.
Speke Bay Lodge, info@ spekebay.com www.speke bay.com Well-located by Lake Victoria and close to the Serengeti's Ndabaka Gate, 125km north of Mwanza on tarmac road.

RUBONDO ISLAND NP
Rubondo Island Camp. Simple lakeside camp (the only option), pleasantly situated at edge of woodland.

Lake Tanganyika
KIGOMA

Kigoma Hilltop, tel (Arusha): 073 297 8879, arusha@ mbalimbali.com www. mbalimbali.com Large four-star hotel overlooking Lake Tanganyika. Water sports, chimpanzee safaris.

Accommodation in Parks
GOMBE STREAM NP
Gombe Forest Lodge, tel: 073 297 8879, arusha@mbalimbali. com www.mbalimbali.com Mid-range lakeshore camp, only option other than basic self-catering *bandas* (huts).

KATAVI PLAINS NP
Chada Katavi Camp, info@ nomad-tanzania.com www. nomad-tanzania.com Small and superb (but not cheap) camp by seasonal Lake Chada.
Katavi Wildlife Camp, katavi_ wildlife@katavi.info www. tanzaniasafaris.info/katavi Excellent little camp, edge of woodlands overlooking flood plain. Owned/operated by long-term Tanzanian residents who know the bush and understand the beauty of simplicity.
Katuma Camp, tel: 073 297 8879, arusha@mbalimbali.com www.mbalimbali.com Very good camp, fine location.

MAHALE MOUNTAINS NP
Zoe's Camp (sometimes known as **Greystoke Mahale**),

info@nomad-tanzania.com www.nomad-tanzania.com Expensive but excellent lake-side camp. Foot safaris in montane forests to observe chimpanzees.
Nkugwe Camp, tel: 073 297 8879, arusha@mbalimbali. com www.mbalimbali.com Slightly cheaper than Zoe's but approaching it in quality, similar location and foot safaris.

WHERE TO EAT

In **Mwanza**, the **Tilapia Hotel** (4 restaurants) and **New Mwanza** serve good food. Independent restaurants include **Kuleana's** (pizza) and **Szechuan** (Chinese). In Kigoma the best restaurant is at the **Hilltop Hotel**.

TOURS AND EXCURSIONS

Rubondo Island NP can be reached by scheduled daily flights from Mwanza. Gombe Stream NP can be reached by boat from Kigoma, as can Mahale Mountains NP (but the latter involves a longish trip unless you go by speed-boat from the Kigoma Hilltop). From Mwanza you can visit the Serengeti NP via its western gate (or by chartered flights). Visits can be arranged from Mwanza to Sukuma Museum, to see cultural artefacts and Sukuma snake dancing.

USEFUL CONTACTS

Mwanza code: 028
Mwanza airport: 028 256 0067; **Aga Khan Hospital (Mwanza):** tel: 028 250 2474.

6
The South

Formerly known as 'The Hell Run', the **Tanzam Highway** from Dar es Salaam to Zambia passes through some of the most beautiful scenery in Tanzania. The road is now quite good, and the journey along it much less harrowing.

Bypassing the lovely **Uluguru Mountains** and the little town of **Morogoro**, the highway proceeds through **Mikumi National Park**. It then climbs through the Rubeho Mountains, dips through the scenic Ruaha Gorge, along the northern border of the **Udzungwa Mountains National Park**, then climbs again to the southern highlands plateau. Skirting the steep ridge on which the small but pleasant town of **Iringa** is perched (and from where yet another magnificent game park, **Ruaha**, is easily accessed), it rolls on towards **Mbeya** and the Zambian border.

Other than those travelling to or from Malawi and Zambia, few tourists travel down this highway, and yet much of the country through which it passes or to its south and north, embraces some of the world's finest wildlife sanctuaries, and some of its loveliest landscapes.

THE MOROGORO REGION

The country between Dar es Salaam and Morogoro is unremarkable for the first 160km (100 miles). At about this point the **Uluguru Mountains** become visible, lending grandeur to an already improving landscape. The mountains, rising to 2646m (8679ft), form part of the Eastern Arc, a broken series of ancient crystalline ranges which

CLIMATE

Generally the area follows the typical climatic patterns of the East African plateau. Days are hot while nights and mornings can be pleasantly cool (especially during the dry season). The greatest threat to travel in the southern game sanctuaries is continual heavy rain. This is most likely from mid-March to mid-May, and to a lesser extent from mid-October to December. At these times certain tracks become impassable and certain airstrips inaccessible.

◀ *Opposite: The Ruaha River and Ruaha National Park, near Msembe.*

93

▶ *Right: A baobab at sunset by the Ruaha River, home to crocodile, hippo and many water birds.*

Don't Miss

*** Selous Game Reserve: great variety of game (including wild dogs) and bird life. Boat safaris.

*** Ruaha National Park: another huge and beautiful wilderness with many big game species (including wild dogs and leopards) and birds.

** Mikumi National Park: five hours' drive from Dar es Salaam. Lion, leopard, elephant.

** Mufundi Area: tea estates, golf course, lovely climate and scenery, nearby Highland Lodge, superbly situated and offering horse riding, fishing and much more.

** Udzungwa National Park: beautiful montane forests rich in endemic species, fine scenery.

curves up from south-central Tanzania, reaching almost to Kilimanjaro. On the ridges are the attractive hamlets of the Luguru people, small clusters of thatched huts often perched at the very end of the high spurs.

Morogoro *

Beneath the northerly slopes of the Uluguru snuggles the town of Morogoro. Its attractiveness owes much to the mountains, as the charm it had in German times and for some time afterwards has largely gone to seed. However, it has a lively **market**, a pleasant little rock garden and an increasing number of reasonable hotels. Morogoro also

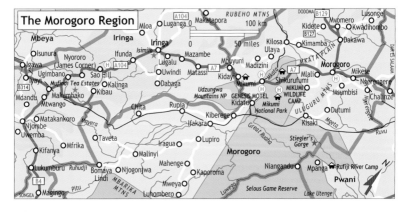

boasts a very testing nine-hole golf course located by the newly renovated Morogoro Hotel, which acts as the 19th hole. And there are signs of an economic upturn in the town's fortunes. There is a flourishing **agricultural college** just outside the town, and a variety of vegetables are grown on the nearby farms. Much of this produce goes to market in Dar es Salaam. Wheat, millet, sugar cane and tobacco are among the area's other crops, as well as sisal.

The town was the scene of fierce fighting during World War I, when the German forces, attacked by the British, put up stern resistance before beating a strategic retreat through the Ulugurus.

Mikumi National Park **

About 80km (50 miles) southwest of Morogoro, the highway bisects Mikumi National Park. It is the fourth largest national park in Tanzania, a fact which surprises many visitors, as the area they frequent is relatively small, encompassing the flood plains of the unimposing but important **Mkata River**, which flows through the park from south to north.

Surrounded on three sides by attractive mountains and hills, the park has a quiet but compelling beauty. During and just after the rains the flood plain can be as green as an Irish meadow, though the autumnal colours of the miombo woodland seen towards the end of the

---

MONEY GROWING ON TREES

- **Sisal** is a species of agave, introduced to the old German East Africa from Mexico. Hairy white string, rope and mats are made from the fibrous leaves, and at one time the industry was a money-spinner. These days labour-intensive plantations and the use of synthetic fibres have reduced demand.
- Handicrafts displayed on the stumps of trees alongside the main road at the village of Mangae, between Morogoro and Mikumi National Park, are woven by women from the fronds of the young **hyphaene palm**. Anyone purchasing mats or baskets is indirectly helping Mikumi, as the villagers begin to see the value, to themselves as well as their country, of tourism.

▼ *Below: The rustic simplicity of Mikumi Wildlife Camp, in the underrated Mikumi National Park.*

African legend has it that God planted the spongy-barked baobab upside down, as its branches look like roots. Another story says that anyone rash enough to pluck one of the baobab's beautiful white flowers will soon afterwards be devoured by a lion (the flowers smell of carrion, and are said to be pollinated by bats and inhabited by malevolent spirits). And as if that wasn't enough, the roasted seeds of the baobab are believed to make a man attractive – not to women – but to crocodiles. The life span of man means little to the tree itself – baobabs with a diameter of 8m (11ft) may well be over 1000 years old.

dry season on the slopes of the hills are deceptive – the leaves are not dying but coming to life, in anticipation of the rains.

The variety of the vegetation is matched by the diversity of animals. Mikumi has many elephants (mostly small, as elephants go), and wild dog and leopard are sometimes seen, though the dogs are sporadic visitors. Lion are commonly encountered, as are giraffe, buffalo, zebra, buck, hippo and warthog. Birdlife is abundant.

The light is often superb, and this, together with the park's natural beauty, make it a wonderful venue for photographers. Sadly, many animals are killed on the main Tanzania–Zambia highway that bisects the park, though the road can offer some unusual photo opportunities.

Udzungwa Mountains National Park *
The Tanzam highway leaves the western boundary of Mikumi by Mikumi Village. From here, a two-hour drive to the south takes travellers alongside the picturesque Udzungwa mountains and to the entrance of the equally picturesque national park of the same name. Gazetted in 1992, the sanctuary enjoys a growing reputation due to its rare endemic plants and animals. Game viewing and bird watching can be enormously rewarding, but neither

▼ *Below: Ruaha (Tanzania) Red-billed Hornbill, preening.*

are easy and visitors should be prepared for some stiff walking and scrambling. Among recent exciting discoveries are the Sanje crested mangabey (a monkey) and a previously unknown francolin, very similar to the hill partridge of the Chinese Himalaya. Despite its rare animal and plant life, Udzungwa's most popular attraction is the Sanje waterfall, from the top of which hikers are treated to glorious views across the northern Kilombero Valley and the Selous. Simple but reasonable accommodation is available in Sanje Village and near the park headquarters. There are three camp sites within the park.

The Ruaha Gorge *

Beyond Mikumi village the Tanzam highway climbs up through the Rubeho Mountains, before descending to follow the course of the Ruaha River, affording, at one point, fine views down the Ruaha Gorge.

The gorge's rock-strewn river is commanded by steep slopes to the south and more gradual slopes to the north, covered by **baobabs**. In the dry season, in sharp light, their bulbous trunks and angular filigree of brances shine silver-white, enhancing the baobab's reputation, among many Africans, as being inhabited by ghosts. There is a pleasant camp site in this 'Baobab Valley', alongside the river.

IRINGA

Beyond this world of spirits lies the plateau country around Iringa, capital of the Southern Highlands. Its situation atop a steep-sided ridge was strategic, as the Germans (who were largely responsible for the town's development) were well aware.

The people of the area, the **Hehe**, helped to stem the southerly expansion of the Maasai in the 19th century, and in 1889, under their formidable chief **Mkwawa**, ambushed a German-led military column as it approached from Morogoro. Using spears and other simple weapons the Hehe slaughtered almost half the German contingent, capturing guns and ammunition. Five years later Mkwawa's unfinished fort at Kalenga, 32km (20 miles) down the Ruaha track from Iringa, was attacked and the Hehe routed.

Iringa's grisly history is implicit in the names of two hills which overlook the town. One, Lundamatwe, means 'Collection of Skulls', the other, Tagamenda, 'Throw Cloths'. The slopes of the former were once festooned with the severed heads of enemy warriors, those of the latter with the clothes of the Hehe dead.

DEATH OF MKWAWA, CHIEF OF THE HEHE

Chief Mkwawa was a renowned freedom fighter, and it is believed that the name of his tribe came from his battle cry, a blood-curdling 'hee-hee'. After the German-led attack upon his fort at Kalenga in 1894, he fled, fighting a guerilla campaign from the hills. The Germans put a price on his head but it was only four years later, in 1898, that the same head was shattered by a bullet. Mkwawa, cornered, shot himself rather than face the inevitable hangman. His opponents, for reasons best known to themselves, had the head hacked off and shipped to Germany. In 1954 the much-travelled skull returned to Kalenga, courtesy of the German government, and is now on display in the small museum there.

SAUCY HOT SPOT OF THE SOUTH

If Iringa's wonderful array of vegetables are sometimes boiled to death in distant hotels, tourists need only grumble about the culinary legacy of the British, and reach for the Dabaga sauce. This chilli sauce (and various other delicious sauces and pickles) is produced in Dabaga, a market-garden area some 30km (20 miles) southeast of Iringa Town. Among Tanzanians, whether at home or far over-seas, Dabaga almost has a cult following. It might not turn a bland meal into cordon-bleu, but it is capable of putting life (and fire) into last week's lettuce or today's boiled beef. On a camping safari, it is worth its weight in gold.

The Germans were forced out by the British during World War I, but Iringa retains the air of a dilapidated Bavarian market town. Traces of its old beauty are still apparent, with its lovely jacarandas, its avenues of eucalyptus and pine, and the occasional show of exotic flowers. It even has a Railway Hotel, a rather odd thing to find at the top of a 200ft-high escarpment and 80km (50 miles) from the nearest railway.

Isimila *

About 23km (14 miles) west of Iringa is one of the most important archeological sites in Africa, Isimila. Stone tools, such as hand-axes, cleavers and hammers, used some 60,000 years ago by people of the Acheulean Age, have been found in abundance, together with the bones of elephants, antelopes and pigs. Some of the bones bear the slash-marks of butchery, and some belonged to creatures now extinct, including ancient evolutionary off-shoots of the giraffe and hippo lines (the ancient hippo, *gorgops*, had eyes on stalks, a little like a crab). Not far from the site are some arresting rock stacks rising to a height of 15m (50ft).

Ruaha National Park ***

Ruaha, recently extended to cover 20,226 km² (7809 sq miles), is now Tanzania's largest national park, and one of its most splendid. The park's headquarters, at **Msembe**, is 130km (80 miles) west of Iringa, along a good dirt track, which passes a series of Hehe villages.

▶▶ *Opposite: Tea pickers performing their highly selective task on the estates at Mufindi in the attractive Southern Highlands.*
▶ *Right: Stone Age tools from the important site at Isimila, near Iringa.*

The famous East African ornithologist John Williams once said of Ruaha that 'of all the East African faunal preserves it is the park of the future'. More than a quarter of a century later his prophecy is beginning to come true, as this glorious wilderness becomes better known and developed.

The **Ruaha River** and its tributaries (some of them 'sand rivers' for the greater part of the year) are the focal points for most visitors, as they are for many animals. Along these watercourses grow wild figs, tamarinds, palms and the lovely winterthorn trees *Faidherbia albida*, all of which provide food and shade for the animals, and which give greener definition to the often dry, always magnificent landscapes.

Parts of the land are dominated by baobabs, though in general the country is covered by *Combretum* and *Commiphora* woodland, with a scattering of acacia. Here and there are open areas of black-cotton grassland, where ostriches, Grant's gazelle and sometimes lion and cheetah might be found.

Ruaha is usually open throughout the year, and is wonderfully green during and just after the rains.

Mufindi Tea Estates ★★

A wonderful complement to a safari in Ruaha is a visit to Mufindi, which is about 100km (60 miles) southwest of Iringa. After the rigours of the bush, the relative comforts

RUAHA SAFARI

Some of the highlights are:
- **Elephant:** Ruaha is renowned for its huge bull elephants, though poaching is once again a serious threat. Family groups are often seen bathing or crossing the river at suitable places.
- **Roan antelope:** sometimes encountered in the low hills close to Msembe or when coming down to drink in the Ruaha River Camp area.
- **Greater kudu:** quite common in many parts of the park.
- **Crocodile** and **hippo:** found in various reaches of the river, including the so-called 'Hippo Pool' close to the bridge which takes visitors into the park.
- **Bird life:** seen throughout the Park, though the river drive is one of the best areas. Species include the rare Eleonora's Falcon (a passage migrant) and Tanzania (Ruaha) Red-billed Hornbill.
- **Wild dog:** wide-ranging and unpredictable but Ruaha is one of their strongholds.
- **Mdonya woodlands:** superb natural botanical gardens, with big game (including leopard) thrown in.

THE SOUTH

Eight members of the beautiful bee-eater family might be seen in The Selous. One of them, Boehm's Bee-eater, is quite uncommon, but might be easily observed and photographed in the Rufiji River Camp, where it nests. The nest is little more than a tunnel in the ground, sometimes astonishingly close to a well-used footpath. Patrons of the camp can be quite alarmed when a slender, bottle-green missile comes hurtling from its underground 'silo' to perch on a nearby branch, awaiting the next unfortunate bee (which the birds devenom by holding them in their bill and rubbing them against a branch).

and cool climate of the highlands are a rest cure for both body and soul.

The tea estates at Mufindi are interesting, with a pleasing geometric beauty. Guided tours around the processing factory can be arranged, but it is the adjacent golf course, a soothing green after the scorched fairways at the coast, and the forest and fishing lakes, which attract most visitors. The nearby Fox's Highland Lodge provides a welcoming and wonderful base.

SELOUS GAME RESERVE

The Selous (pronounced 'Sell-oo') is the oldest and biggest game reserve in Africa and among one of the wildest sanctuaries on earth. The reserve extends over more than 50,000km² (19,300 sq miles) of miombo woodland, terminalia thicket, open grassland and gallery forest, watered by the **Rufiji River**, its network of tributaries, and its ox-bow lakes. Very few travellers venture into the almost trackless wastes south of the Rufiji, and those who do must be entirely self-sufficient. Until recently the reserve's northern sector, quite large and wild in itself, was the only one developed for tourism. Elsewhere the

▶▶ *Opposite: Boat safari helmsmen and game scouts on Lake Tagalala in Selous Game Reserve.*
▶ *Right: The Rufiji River, which waters the huge wilderness of the Selous Game Reserve.*

reserve is divided into hunting blocks. Sadly, elephant poaching in the Selous is again a serious menace.

Northern Selous: Eastern Sector

The drive to the Selous from Dar es Salaam, southwards along about 130km (80 miles) of recently laid tarmac to Kibiti, and 105km (66 miles) of dirt track beyond that passes, in its latter stages, through a series of simple villages. Several basic camps are situated outside the Reserve's northeastern gate at Mtemere, and a little way beyond the gate is **Rufiji River Camp**, long popular with expatriates.

The river from which it takes its name captures the imagination, and a boat safari, through pods of wallowing hippo and past basking crocodiles, is the highlight of any Selous safari for most people. Buffalo, waterbuck, and impala can usually be seen in the water meadows. Giraffes have not yet found their way across the Rufiji, but might be seen on the northern banks, while elephant and lion are always possibilities. Water birds are plentiful, and include the African skimmer, kingfishers, goliath heron and the nocturnal Pel's fishing owl.

In some places the river banks are lined by avenues of headless borassus palms, their spindle-shaped boles like regiments of giant aliens. Against a Selous sunset, the river glittering with fragmented light and the Uluguru Mountains

WHISTLING THORN

The whistling thorn (*Acacia drepanolobium*) is covered in natural galls, or lesions, and, like all acacias, by sharp thorns. It gets its name from the sound made by the wind as it passes over the tiny holes in the hollow galls, and from the vibration the wind causes in the slender thorns. The galls are inhabited by creatures such as cremogaster ants, which gain some protection from the acacia's thorns, and which, in turn, are thought to deter some animals from browsing on the foliage. When the foliage dies off, the intricate mass of silver-grey galls and spiky branches has a fierce and abstract beauty.

TOURS AND EXCURSIONS

Morogoro
Walks in Uluguru Mountains, birding, nine-hole golf course.

Iringa Area
Mkwawa Museum, Kalenga. Dedicated to Hehe chief. **Mufindi Tea Estates & golf course** (150km SW). Good birding, highland climate. Closer to Iringa is the interesting **Isimila Stone Age site**.

Mbeya
Many mountain walks plus Kitulo NP (wildflowers). Best December to April.

blue-grey in the distance, the palms make a fantastic sight. From their bare tops, here and there along the river, fish eagles throw back their snow-white heads and send their evocative call echoing along the waterway.

The bush around the Rufiji River Camp is almost as interesting, with mature miombo woodland close by, reminding northern visitors of the broad-leaved woodlands of home, and less familiar tracts of whistling thorn beyond. Wild dogs, elephants and other animals might sometimes be seen in the shady miombo woodland, with giraffes, greater kudu, eland, zebra and wildebeest often among the whistling thorn. In the dry season they file through the acacias to drink at the river, or the attractive little Lake Mzizima, a short drive from the camp.

Northern Selous: East-Central Sector

A leisurely one-and-a-half hour's drive or so from Rufiji River brings the traveller to the centre of a delightful area of *Terminalia spinosa* parkland and waterside terraces which, after the rains, are beautifully lush and green. Plentiful water and grazing attract a variety of wildlife, including lion, leopard, wild dog and many bird species, and as elsewhere boat safaris are recommended. Among the camps and lodges serving this prime game-viewing area are **Selous Safari**, **Impala** and **Lake Manze**, all on the Rufiji or adjacent lakes.

◀ *Left: Endangered because of their susceptibility to diseases borne by domesticated canines, sightings of wild dog have become a highlight of safaris in the southern national parks.*

◀◀ *Opposite: One of the Rufiji River's many hippos takes to the water after a night's grazing on the banks.*

Northern Selous: West-Central Sector

West of the Mbuyu area the *Terminalia* woodland degenerates into scrub as the land rises towards Beho-Beho, an expanse of hilly terrain and open grassland which Dr Alan Rodgers, one of the greatest authorities on the Selous, has described as 'some of the most magnificent wildlife country in East Africa'. Many game animals, including lion, wild dogs and hyenas, seem to agree with him. Elephant are often seen in the groves of doum palm alongside watercourses or sand rivers, and sable antelope inhabit the wooded hills in the northwest.

Rhino, once common in the area, still survive in small numbers but are rarely seen, while hippo and crocodiles are present in the river system and in **Lake Tagalala**.

Bird life is abundant on and around the rivers and the lake, as well as throughout the grasslands, bush and riverine woodland.

Other attractions in this **West-Central sector** include the **hot springs**, a pretty picnic spot where you may bathe or swim in the warm waters, **Stiegler's Gorge** (on the Rufiji), and **Selous' grave**, close to Beho-Beho Camp. Among the old trenches overlooking the spot where Selous met his death, rifle cartridges may still be discovered. Visitors to the reserve still sometimes place wild

FOOT SAFARIS

In the Selous, as in other game reserves (but **not** most National Parks), visitors can experience some of the thrills of old-time safaris by walking, rather than driving, through the bush, accompanied by an armed game scout. Such safaris can be disappointing for photographers of big game, as animals will usually avoid people on foot and vanish into the vegetation. Now and again, however, lions, elephants or buffalo remain unaware of approaching humans, allowing for an exciting encounter. Such encounters are rarely dangerous but participants should be aware that accidents do occasionally occur. Big game or not, a foot safari allows participants a fascinating insight into life in the bush, where the spoor of a jackal, the glimpse of a wild flower, the smell of a dead antelope, or the sound of a snapping twig can arouse a whole spectrum of emotions, including wonder – and fear.

SACRED SCARABS

There are various species of scarab beetle, or as they are more prosaically known, dung beetles. The scarab was sacred to the ancient Egyptians, who perhaps recognized its enterprise and industry. During or immediately after the rains, the beetles can often be seen paddling balls of buffalo or elephant dung across the tracks, using their back pair of legs. The female beetle, after burying the ball of dung in a suitable spot, lays her eggs in it. The resulting grub enters the world surrounded by what (to them) is an irresistible and seemingly inexhaustible supply of food.

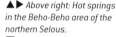 ▲▶ *Above right: Hot springs in the Beho-Beho area of the northern Selous.*
▼ *Below: Sand Rivers Lodge, overlooking the Rufiji River, Selous Game Reserve.*

flowers on the grave in sentimental but sincere tribute, using beer bottles as vases (Selous, who was teetotal, might not have approved).

Camps and lodges in the west-central sector include **Sand Rivers**, on the Rufiji; the long-established **Beho-Beho Camp**, on the slopes of a hill above a small tributary of the Beho-Beho River; **Mivumo River Lodge**, on the Rufiji by Steigler's Gorge; and, in more remote western corners, **Selous Luxury Camp**, by a water hole, and **Amara Selous**, close to the Ruaha/Rufiji confluence.

BEST TIMES TO VISIT

Mid-May to mid-Oct dry, cool mornings and evenings. Rain usually mid-Oct to mid-May, peaking Mar–Apr; can restrict travel on certain tracks in parks.

GETTING THERE

Most tourists fly into Dar or Zanzibar by international flights and onwards by internal flights or by safari company vehicles from Dar.

WHERE TO STAY

Morogoro

Hotel Oasis, tel: 023 261 4178, hoteloasistz@morogoro. net www.hoteloasistz.com Pleasant hotel close to town centre. Swimming pool.

Iringa

Old Farmhouse, Kisolanza, tel: 075 430 6144, info@kiso lanza.com www.kisolanza. com Pleasant stop-over, 50km (30 miles) southwest of Iringa.

Mbeya

Mt Livingstone Hotel, tel: 025 250 3334, infomlh@yahoo. com www.twiga.ch/TZ/mt livingstone.htm Very reasonable place, town centre.

Mikumi NP

Stanley's Kopje Camp, info@ tanzaniasafaris.info www. tanzaniasafaris.info Secluded tented camp set around a rocky outcrop.
Vuma Hills Lodge, info@tanza niasafaris.info www.tanzania safaris.info Among wooded hills south of Dar-Zambia highway.

Mikumi Wildlife Camp, tel: 068 399 9445, reservations@ mikumiwildlifecamp.com www.mikumiwildlifecamp.com Popular, long-established camp overlooking flood plain.

Ruaha NP

Kwihala Camp, tel: 022 245 2005/6, reservations@kwihala. com www.adventurecamps tz.com Superb, small, simple camp in excellent area.
Mwagusi Safari Lodge, tel (USA toll free): 1 800 423 4236, info@kerdowney.com www.kerdowney.com One of Ruaha's best up-market safari options, by a sand river.
Mdonya Old River Camp, tel: 022 245 2005/6, mdonya@ adventurecampstz.com www.adventurecampstz.com Simple camp in woodlands. Leopards often encountered, sometimes wild dogs.
Ruaha River Lodge, info@tan zaniasafaris.info www.tanza niasafaris.info Quite large but simple, popular, reasonably priced camp.

Selous Game Reserve

Selous Safari Camp, tel: 022 212 8485, www.selous.com Up-market camp in prime game area.
Lake Manze Tented Camp, tel: 022 245 2005/6, manze@ adventurecampstz.com www. lakemanze.com Refreshingly simple camp in core game area. Lions, wild dogs often seen. Boat safaris.
Selous Impala Camp, tel: 022 245 2005/6, info@adventure campstz.com www.adventure

campstz.com Perhaps best all-round option in the Selous.
Rufiji River Camp, info@tanza niasafaris.info www.tanzania safaris.info Long-time favourite with 'old Africa hands'. Game drives, boat safaris.
Beho Beho Camp, tel: +44 (0)193 226 0618, reservations @behobeho.com www.beho beho.com Away from river but overlooking undulating grasslands and hills. Hippo pool nearby, boat trips on lake.
Sand Rivers Selous, info@ nomad-tanzania.com www. nomad-tanzania.com Little way from key game areas but a wonderful, elegant camp on the river. Annexe (Kiba Point) is available to private groups.

Udzungwa NP

Udzungwa Falls Lodge, tel: 075 830 5630, info@udzun gwafallslodge.com www. udzungwafallslodge.com Reasonable hotel with swimming pool, close to popular Sanje Falls trail.
Twiga Hotel, tel: 023 262 0224, udzungwa@gmail.com www.udzungwa.org Basic but adequate hotel by park entrance, Mang'ula.

WHERE TO EAT

Most visitors eat in the lodges, hotels, etc.

USEFUL CONTACTS

Flying Doctor (Dar): tel: 022 550 3833, info@dsmflying doctors.com Good website for lodge/camp reviews is www.tanzania odyssey.com

7
Zanzibar, Pemba and Mafia

Forty kilometres (25 miles) east of Bagamoyo, off the mid-Tanzanian coast, lies the island of Unguja or, as it is more commonly known to westerners, Zanzibar Island. It is only 85km (53 miles) long and 20km (12 miles) wide, but for centuries its importance has been out of all proportion to its size. In the 19th century it was said that 'when the flute is played in Zanzibar, they dance at the lakes', a tribute to the far-reaching powers of the Omani Sultans who made Zanzibar the seat of their Imamate, and their home. It was the earlier sultans, particularly **Said the Great**, founder of the Zanzibar sultanate in 1832, who brought prosperity to the islands, largely by encouraging the planting of cloves, promoting the slave trade on which the plantations depended, and importing ivory.

But there is much more to Unguja, and its sister island **Pemba**, away to the north, than history. They are low-lying, with no significant mountains or rivers, but they are pleasant, fertile places, their sultry air still heavy, at times, with the scent of spices.

A BRIEF HISTORY OF ZANZIBAR

The early history of the islands remains obscure, although they were mentioned in *The Periplus of the Erythrean Sea*, a seafarers' guide written by a **Greek** merchant in AD 60. It is fairly certain that **Arabs** had begun to settle in Zanzibar by the 9th century, and that 400 years later **Shirazi Persians** made their home there. By 1045 the indigenous population had already adopted Islam. Zanzibar's first

◀ *Opposite: The old Arab fort and the House of Wonders (behind) in Stone Town.*

107

mosque, at Kizimkazi, was built in 1107. The Persians and Arabs passed on commercial know-how as well as genes, inspiring vigorous trade with countries as far afield as China. This buoyant interchange was depressed by two centuries of **Portuguese** rule, beginning in 1500. But by 1700 the Portuguese were in retreat, ousted by the resurgent **Omani Arabs**.

Omani rule along the coast soon became absolute, though there were many feuds among the powerful families, and a few indigenous chiefs retained power in the

▶ *Opposite: The crumbling house of Tippu Tip, best known of Zanzibar's slave traders.*

▼ *Below: Graves at Zanzibar's first mosque, the 12th-century house of worship at Kizimkazi.*

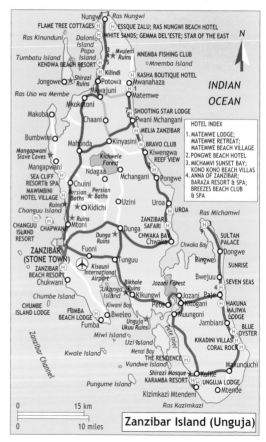

Zanzibar Island (Unguja)

HOTEL INDEX
1. MATEMWE LODGE; MATEMWE RETREAT; MATEMWE BEACH VILLAGE
2. PONGWE BEACH HOTEL
3. MICHAMVI SUNSET BAY; KONO KONO BEACH VILLAS
4. ANNA OF ZANZIBAR; BARAZA RESORT & SPA; BREEZES BEACH CLUB & SPA

remoter areas. But Zanzibar's rise to fame – and notoriety – really began in 1832, when **Sultan Seyid Said** (Said the Great) chose to control his extensive Imamate from Zanzibar rather than Muscat, the Omani capital on the Arabian peninsula

Capital of the Slave Trade

On the death of Said in 1856, the Omani sultanate broke away from Zanzibar. By then Zanzibar and Pemba were well on the way to prosperity, based on the dramatic expansion of the **clove** plantations, and the equally dramatic expansion of the **ivory** and **slave trades**.

The slave trade had existed for centuries before the sultans came to Zanzibar, but not on such a terrible and escalating scale. The British, who had established an early presence in Zanzibar, opposed the trade and, through their political agents, notably **Atkins Hamerton** and **John Kirk**, gained the confidence of the two most influential sultans of the period, Said and his son **Barghash**. The British were instrumental in limiting and finally ending the slave trade, though it was almost 50 years after the closing of the infamous Zanzibar slave market, in 1873, that slavery was completely eradicated from mainland Tanganyika.

TIPPU TIP

The best known of all Zanzibari slave traders was Tippu Tip (his real name was Hamed Bin Muhammed El Murjebi). He was ruthless and determined, but also a man of intelligence, ability and courage. On one occasion, when hit by three arrows during a skirmish, he turned on his assailants and, together with his companions, killed more than 1000 within an hour. Stanley regarded him as 'the most remarkable man I had met among the Arabs, Waswahili and the half-castes in Africa', and the slaver, with a personal retinue of 96 (including his 35 wives and concubines) sailed from Zanzibar to West Africa as part of Stanley's final expedition in 1887. Tippu Tip enjoyed retirement as a wealthy and respected gentleman, in his house in Zanzibar Town. The house still stands.

BRITAIN'S MAN IN ZANZIBAR

John Kirk was, perhaps, the best known of several very able British consuls attached to Zanzibar. A former travelling partner of Livingstone's and a friend and advisor of Sultan Barghash, his influence was enormous. He helped to end the slave trade, and also assisted various explorers (although Stanley detested him). His house at Mbweni, just south of Zanzibar town, and built for him by Barghash, still stands, though on private land. Sadly it is being allowed to crumble. It was here that Kirk, an expert botanist, lovingly created an experimental garden, introducing improved varieties of native food-plants and trees, and other plants likely to prove of economical value to the islands.

The Explorers

From the late 1850s to the mid-1870s, up to 30,000 slaves a year were brought to Zanzibar. Throughout the same period, a series of extraordinary men were heading in the opposite direction. **Burton** and **Speke** passed through Zanzibar in 1857, to seek the source of the Nile which Speke discovered on his second attempt in 1862, accompanied by Grant. In 1866 **Livingstone** set out from Zanzibar on his last journey, returning (in a coffin) in 1874. In 1872 **H.M. Stanley** sailed into Zanzibar to a hero's welcome after his historic meeting with Livingstone in Ujiji.

The explorers were often helped by the Zanzibari slave traders, who, however ruthless, regarded slaving as legitimate business. The sultans, too, would have been puzzled by western moralities, not least because of American and European involvement in the West African slave trade. They signed anti-slavery legislation only under pressure, but the benefits which the sultans brought to Zanzibar should not be overlooked. Their legacy included a thriving economy, which the clove plantations easily sustained long after the decline of the slave trade, telegraph and shipping links with Europe, and in Zanzibar Town a clean water supply.

Revolution

Zanzibar became a British protect-orate in 1890, and for more than 70 years enjoyed relative peace and prosperity. Apart from a brief naval action at the start of World War I, when the German battle cruiser *Koenigsberg* shelled and sank the British warship *Pegasus* in Zanzibar harbour, the islands were not directly affected by the two world wars. As soon as the British left, however, *Pax Britannica* left on the same tide. In 1963 **Sayyid Jamshid Bin Abdulla Bin Khalif**, the last of the Zanzibari sultans, came to the throne. In January 1964, one month after Zanzibar's independence, he was overthrown in a bloody revolution. About 13,000 people, mostly Arabs, were slaughtered in an orgy of killing. A generation later, peace (if not political stability) has returned to the islands, which are beginning to recover some of their former auto-nomy and prosperity, and to attract more tourists.

▲ *Above: The gazebo in Jamituri Gardens on Stone Town's seafront.*
◀ *Opposite: 'Livingstone's House', Zanzibar. The house was, in fact, made available to the explorer by Sultan Majid.*

THE STONE TOWN

The Stone Town is Zanzibar's old quarter. It has been called 'the only functioning historical city in East Africa' and is so little changed since the 1850s (at least structurally) that Burton and Speke, it seems, might just have left for the interior. The best way to appreciate this is to walk, as the explorers did, through the old streets.

Seafront

There are no prescribed routes for a tour of Stone Town – but perhaps the seafront is an appropriate place to start. People arriving by sea will pass the old dhow harbour as they leave the dockside complex. The great ocean-going dhows are mostly gone, but visitors should see smaller *jahazi* or *mashua*, still common and basically unchanged throughout the years. At sea, lateen sails silhouetted against a flaming sunset, their romantic appeal can still be captivating. Smaller dhows are still common.

> **THE FACES OF STONE TOWN**
>
> The faces of most Zanzibaris are a living documentary of the island's cosmopolitan past, while their clothes are an indication of their devotion to Islam. Traditional *kanzu*, an ankle-length robe worn by men, and *bui-bui*, the long black gown worn by women, are not as evident as they were, but the embroidered caps favoured by Muslim men are still popular, and many women still regard the world through large and beautiful dark eyes, enhanced by *kohl*, all other features screened from the gaze of men by a headscarf (the *hijab*) and the flowing *bui-bui*.

DOORWAYS TO HISTORY

Zanzibar doors have become renowned. Custom ordained that the doorway of a house should be built before the house itself, presumably to exert a benign influence over the completed building. The ritual was given added strength by Koranic scripts and representational carvings which adorn the doorways. The Zanzibar door was traditionally made of teak, and was set in a square frame, covered by delicate and slender carvings. Indian influences during the 19th century modified this prototype, producing doors with arched tops and more elaborate floral designs. Motifs to be seen on such doors include the lotus (symbol of reproductive power), the fish (fertility), the chain (security) and the frankincense tree (wealth).

A short distance from the dockyard gate Mizingani Road begins its southwesterly course along one of the most historic seafronts in the world. Near its northern end is the ornately attractive **Ismaili Dispensary** (now a cultural centre) presented to the Aga Khan's followers in Zanzibar on the occasion of Queen Victoria's Jubilee. A little further along the road, still heading southwest, is the former Sultan's Palace, now the **People's Palace**, and open to the public. First occupied by a reigning sovereign in 1911, it previously accommodated members of the royal family and harem. In the graveyard alongside, Said the Great and other sultans lie buried. The interior of the palace is comfortably rather than splendidly furnished, but it provides interesting insights into a vanished and exotic period of Zanzibar's history.

Adjacent to the palace is the **House of Wonders**, the *Beit el-Ajaib*, built by Sultan Barghash in 1883. Together with the original palace it was damaged by shell-fire during a scuffle for the accession in 1896, when British warships intervened, precipitating 'the shortest war in history' (it lasted for 45 minutes). The Beit el-Ajaib has now become a museum, minus the lions and the other animals which were once kept caged outside its gates. It contains the most beautiful examples of 'Zanzibar doors' in East Africa.

▶ *Right: The House of Wonders, built as a ceremonial palace in 1883 by Sultan Barghash.*

A little further down the seafront stands the **Arab Fort**. It withstood an attack by the Mazrui Arabs from Mombasa in 1754, and was afterwards used as a gaol. Criminals were once publicly beheaded just outside its walls, though nowadays happier events, such as musical concerts, take place in the fort's amphitheatre. A popular café, with adjacent souvenir stalls, lies alongside the amphitheatre.

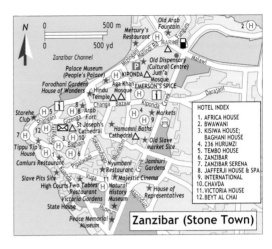

Zanzibar (Stone Town)

HOTEL INDEX
1. AFRICA HOUSE
2. BWAWANI
3. KISIWA HOUSE; BAGHANI HOUSE
4. 236 HURUMZI
5. TEMBO HOUSE
6. ZANZIBAR
7. ZANZIBAR SERENA
8. JAFFERJI HOUSE & SPA
9. INTERNATIONAL
10. CHAVDA
11. VICTORIA HOUSE
12. BEYT AL CHAI

Enclosed by a promontory to the west of the fort is the district known as Shangani, 'The Place of Beads'. The original **slave market** (in the square now overlooked by the Serena Hotel) once stood here and, appropriately, the house of **Tippu Tip**, most notorious of the Zanzibar slavers, can be found nearby, in a shadowy, seldom-visited corner of the town.

A few doors away is the **Africa House Hotel**, a less ominous building with its own nostalgia. Formerly British Club, it clings, with stiff upper lip, to its colonial past. Its seaward-facing terrace is popular at sundown. The **Zanzibar Hotel**, in the same district, is another interesting old building, its rooms traditionally constructed from mangrove poles. The poles, impervious to termites, are still used throughout East Africa, and their export to the Gulf and elsewhere, by dhow, is one of the oldest forms of trade in the region.

In the southern area of Stone Town is the **National Museum**, now virtually derelict within. At the back of the museum is the oldest carved door in Stone Town. Close by on Kaunda Road are the **High Courts**, with their blend of Arabic and Portuguese styles, and the **State House**. All three buildings were designed by the British architect John Sinclair, much influenced by the East and Islam.

FINDING YOUR WAY IN STONE TOWN

- **Walking** is undoubtedly the best (and often only) way to negotiate the fascinating narrow streets of Stone Town.
- **Guides** are not essential, but the best of them, often older, know their town and its absorbing history. Visitors should ask for a guide at their hotel or any tourist centre.
- If you choose to discover Stone Town on your own, however, you can 'lose' yourself in the maze of alleyways without too much fear of being lost for long, or of having anything **stolen**, though petty crime is increasing and visitors should use a little common sense (e.g. by not wearing expensive jewellery).
- Don't take **photographs** without asking.
- Please respect Islamic modesty by wearing clothes that are not too revealing.

THE CATHEDRAL

Stone Town's Cathedral Church of Christ, built on the site of the old slave market, is an imposing building. The altar was erected on the same spot as the slave whipping post had been, and a stained-glass window commemorates the British sailors who died on anti-slaving patrols. On a pillar beside the chancel is a crucifix, made from the tree under which Livingstone's heart was buried. Interred behind the cathedral altar are the remains of Bishop Steere, who supervised the building of the cathedral and who, every Friday, had the Victorian cheek to preach to Muslims in the adjoining Chapel of the Blessed Sacrament. This obviously didn't upset the reigning sultan, Barghash, who donated a clock to adorn the Cathedral tower.

Markets Old and Young

Zanzibar's seafront reeks of history, but the true adventure of Stone Town is to lose yourself in its maze of alleyways and high-walled buildings, and experience the day-to-day life of this sometimes squalid, always exciting hotchpotch. Changa Bazaar and Gizenga Street are among the most interesting. Except in the heat of the afternoon the streets bustle with unpretentious enterprise. Many shops now cater for tourists though some traditional *dukas* remain, selling vegetables and fruit or specializing in clocks or simple tailoring, while coffee sellers still weave through the crowds with their pots of 'black adrenalin'.

Close to the town's main markets, just west of Creek Road, is the **Cathedral Church of Christ** which, until 1873, was the site of the infamous slave market. Here, up to 300 slaves or more were herded and paraded each day in the late afternoon and subjected to the most intimate and embarrassing scrutiny. Muscles and teeth were examined, sticks were thrown for the male slaves to retrieve (to test their basic fitness), and the younger, more attractive women were lasciviously fondled.

Zanzibar's Roman Catholic cathedral, **St Joseph's**, on the edge of Shangani, has a less disturbing history. There are mosques too, as one might expect, the most notable being the **Aga Khan**, the **Bohora**, and the **Malindi**. Hinduism is represented by the **Shakti Temple**. Other buildings of interest include the old British Consulate,

◀ *Left: Just a few of the spices and fruits to be seen (and sampled) in Zanzibar.*
◀◀ *Opposite top: Coffee – thick, black and strong.*
◀▼ *Opposite bottom: The Cathedral Church of Christ, founded in 1873 on the slave market.*

where several famous explorers stayed, the Hamamni Persian Baths and, on Kenyatta Road, General Mathews House (now a dental surgery).

The Stone Town might now be devoted to tourism, including Internet centres, but its mysterious, intriguing 19th-century counterpart is never far away.

AROUND UNGUJA ISLAND

Zanzibar's blend of troubled history and relaxing peacefulness can be experienced outside, as well as inside, the Stone Town. So-called **'Spice Tours'** introduce the visitor to the fascinating world of Zanzibar's spice-growing areas, and are usually combined with a history lesson. Tourists will catch some interesting glimpses of life among the villages, with their little mud-and-wattle houses roofed with palm thatch or corrugated iron. And on the roads they might see Indian-style ox-carts or Zanzibar's unique country buses which, with their wooden coachwork, glass-less windows and slatted seats, look more like early 19th-century railway carriages, and are just about as comfortable.

After leaving town, the Spice Tours pass **Livingstone's House**. The missionary-explorer stayed here in 1866 prior to his final expedition. A little further north is **Marahubi Palace**, built by Sultan Barghash to house his harem. He did not live to enjoy his visits there, and 11 years after his death it burned down. It is now in ruins, but ruins can be

SKELETONS – BUT NOT IN THE CUPBOARDS

The custom of burying slaves alive in the walls of houses under construction is thought to have been fairly common in old Zanzibar. Skeletons were discovered in the foundations of the old Cable and Wireless building, erected on the site of the original slave market at Shangani by Sultan Barghash to bring enlightenment to Zanzibar. A more awful irony distinguishes a building called Mambo Msigee on the tip of the Shangani promontory. It was formerly occupied by such anti-slavery luminaries as the Universities Mission to Central Africa and Sir John Kirk, who were all blithely unaware that living slaves had been entombed in the walls which sheltered them.

romantic, and Marahubi's melancholic wistfulness is not unpleasant. Further north still are the ruins of another palace, **Mtoni**, once occupied by Said the Great and his huge household, including his fascinating daughter Salme, whose autobiography, Memoirs of an Arabian Princess, had it been fiction, would have been rejected by most publishers as being too unlikely. The Mtoni Marine Centre next door, which is helping to restore this important monument, organizes 'Princess Salme Tours' and lamp-lit dinners and concerts among the ruins.

Less than 20km (12 miles) to the north of Mtoni is **Mangapwani**. There is a pleasant beach here and two caves. One, the **Coral Cave**, is by the beach itself, the second, the **Slave Cave**, just to the north. The latter was used for holding slaves after 1873, when their export was forbidden. Another place of historical interest north of Zanzibar Town is the **Persian Baths** at Kidichi, built by Sultan Said.

In the centre of Zanzibar Island, at **Dunga**, are the ruins of a fortified palace, former home of a tyrannical local chief. Further south, near Pete, is **Jozani Forest**, a wildlife sanctuary where endemic and endangered Zanzibar red colobus monkeys may be observed. And in the extreme south, some 30km (20 miles) beyond Jozani, travellers will find traces of an old Shirazian settlement by the seashore at **Kizimkazi**. Its mosque was the first to be built on the East African coast (in 1107). Dolphins are found off Kizimkazi and boats are available for visitors who wish to see these unusual mammals.

◄ *Left: Clear, warm waters, for so many one of the attractions of Zanzibar, at Mangapwani, north of Stone Town.*
◄◄ *Opposite: Tourists stop off at Marahubi to see the atmospheric ruins of Sultan Barghash's harem.*

Sea and Shore

Too much history can be cloying and a convenient complement to the past is a day or two in the present, by the sea. Zanzibar's **beaches**, particularly in the north and east ('The Sunrise Coast') are often beautiful and unspoilt, locations for lotus-eating laziness. The villagers along this coast are mostly involved in fishing and seaweed harvesting, though other occupations include cattle raising, mat-making, lime-burning and the making of embroidered Muslim caps.

Another possibility is to take a boat to one of Zanzibar's offshore islets. The most popular of these is commonly known as **Prison** (*Changuu*) Island. Another islet with a sombre name is **Grave** (*Chapwani*) Island. Its name relates to the cemetery there, designated by Sultan Barghash as a graveyard for British sailors killed on anti-slavery patrols, though some graves go back to the early decades of the 19th century. Despite their names, the islands are far from grim, and are known for their beaches, swimming, snorkelling and sunbathing.

PEMBA

Nearly 50km (32 miles) to the north is an island not much smaller than Unguja itself. Pemba, known to the Arabs as *Al Khudra*, the Green Island, is little visited by tourists, although it is now beginning to realize its potential.

PRISON ISLAND

Originally owned by an Arab who detained unruly slaves on it, Prison Island was later bought by Lloyd Mathews, who had a prison built there in 1893. The ruins of the prison (it was never used) have been converted into a hotel and the small island, now privately owned, is an attractive place, with fine beaches and pleasant woodland walks. The woodland is inhabited by tiny suni antelopes, as well as a variety of birds – including introduced peafowl. The animal which arouses most interest, however, is the giant land tortoise, originally from Aldabra. There are about 50 of these huge reptiles, which hiss like snakes when threatened but which are harmless.

Cloves

Like Unguja, Pemba's 19th-century history was dominated by cloves and slaves. Pemba is, in fact, the true island of cloves, and although the industry is declining and prices falling, much of Pemba is still covered by clove trees, some of them a century and a half old. During the harvest season, between July and December, the oily fragrance of cloves drifts over the island in an aromatic mist. Pickers climb the trees, which can attain a height of 15m (50ft), by means of ropes or ladders, snapping off clusters of unopened buds, greenish or yellowish-red in colour. These are collected in baskets and laid out in the sun for four to seven days, until their colour deepens into the familiar dark brown, when they are graded and packed for export. They are eventually, of course, used in cooking and baking, but also in the manufacture of aromatic and medicinal oils, and in Indonesia, to flavour cigarettes.

Around the Island

The many ruins around the island bear testimony to the its older, more general past. At **Chake Chake**, Pemba's principal town, there are remains of a 13th-century Shirazi settlement, a mosque which is said to be one of the finest of its type on the coast of East Africa, and a Muslim fort (now converted into a hospital). At **Pujini**, 11km (7 miles) north of Chake

Chake, there is a 14th-century fortified settlement, and at **Ras Mkumbuu**, an attractive headland on the western coast, the ruins of an Islamic settlement established in the 9th or even 8th century.

Pemba has several endemic animal, bird and plant species, especially in Ngezi Forest in the northwest, but the island is better known for its enchanting marine life. Its dive sites are among the best and most exciting in the world. It also has many little-known beaches, including those on Misali Island, a paradise for snorkellers and divers and former haunt of the pirate Captain Kidd.

MAFIA ISLAND *

Situated 160km (100 miles) south of Zanzibar Island, Mafia is 394km^2 (152 sq miles) in area. It has its own interesting history, and though relatively flat is not un-attractive, but most visitors come to enjoy its beaches and its excellent reputation as a centre for sea-fishing, snorkelling and diving. Its marine park (the first in Tanzania) has been described, by an experienced diver, as 'truly spectacular'. Among the many remarkable marine creatures that are found there or that pass through are whale sharks (October–March).

◀ *Opposite: Drying cloves on Pemba Island, the real 'Isle of Cloves'.*
▼ *Below: The technology of scuba diving mixes with the timelessness of an old dhow off the coast of Zanzibar.*

BEST TIMES TO VISIT

Best mid-May to mid-October. Jan–Mar can be hot and humid, but monsoon breezes often temper the air. Rain in Mar–Apr, and to a lesser extent Nov–Dec, can sometimes be heavy and frustrating.

GETTING THERE

Most tourists not on package-tour flights fly to Dar then to Zanzibar via **local airlines** (e.g. Coastal Air and Zanair). Regular flights also leave Dar for Mafia but check beforehand. **Ferries** operate between Dar and Zanzibar and are usually reliable and safe though two have sunk in recent years.

GETTING AROUND

Stone Town is best appreciated on foot. **Official guides** can be hired via the better hotels. Agree details and itinerary beforehand. **Motor scooters** and **bicycles** can also be hired. **Taxis** are plentiful in Zanzibar Town and **mini-buses** can be booked from the Old Fort to most beach resorts. Polite but firm haggling is advised, with fees agreed before departing. Pemba has fewer choices and you might have to use your initiative and take a **local bus**.

WHERE TO STAY

Zanzibar Town (Stone Town)
Emerson's Spice Hotel, tel: 024 223 2776, reservation@ emersonspice.com www.emer sonspice.com Reinvented by idiosyncratic, style-conscious American. Lavishly decorated, will eventually have 12 rooms (presently four).

Jafferji House and Spa, tel: 077 374 0888, gm@jafferjihouse. net www.jafferjihouse.net Another luxurious, elaborately furnished hotel.
Zanzibar Serena, tel: 024 223 3051, www.serenahotels.com/ serenazanzibar Up-market hotel in excellent location on Shangani seafront.
Tembo House Hotel, tel: 024 223 2069, info@tembohotel. com www.tembohotel.com Furnished in Zanzibar style, fine location on beach/water-front. Old wing preferable. Reasonably priced, no alcohol.

Beach Hotels
AROUND STONE TOWN
Seacliff Resort & Spa, tel: 076 770 2241–9, reservations@sea cliffzanzibar.com www.sea cliffzanzibar.com Up-market, overlooking sea, Mangapwani.
Mtoni Marine Centre, tel: 024 225 0140, mtoni@zanzibar. cc www.mtoni.com Popular, moderately priced beach hotel just north of Stone Town, by Mtoni Palace Ruins. Pleasant alternative to in-town hotels.
Mbweni Ruins Hotel, tel: 077 501 6541 or 076 762 9364, hotel@mbweni.com www. mbweni.com Situated among lovely botanical gardens, by 19th-century ruins, fine beach.

NORTHWEST/NORTH COAST
Kendwa
Gemma del' Est, tel: 024 224 0175, info.sote@diamonds-resorts.com http://lagemma dellest-diamonds-resorts.com Large luxury resort amid tropical gardens, close to Nungwi. Sea views.

Nungwi
Essque Zalu, tel: 077 868 3960, sales@essquehotels.com www.essquehotels.com Five-star boutique resort, fine location, northeast tip of Nungwi.
Ras Nungwi Beach Hotel, tel: 024 223 3767, info@rasnungwi. com www.rasnungwi.com Up-market resort. Solid reputation, on quieter eastern edge of Nungwi Point.
Flame Tree Cottages, tel: 024 224 0100, www.flametreecot tages.com Quiet, respectable, well-managed, good value.

EAST COAST
Matemwe
Mnemba Island Lodge, tel (UK): +44 (0) 20 7471 8780, (USA toll free): 1 866 356 4691, www.mnembaisland.com Super-exclusive, expensive, exceptional. Beautiful beach, superb snorkeling and diving.
Matemwe Lodge, matemwe lodge@asilaafrica.com www. asilaafrica.com/Matemwe-Lodge Consistently popular lodge; twelve comfortable bungalows on a coral outcrop.
Matemwe Retreat, matemwe retreat@asilaafrica.com www. asilaafrica.com/Matemwe-Retreat Sister resort of Matemwe Lodge. Four self-contained 'retreats', ideal for honeymooners.
Matemwe Beach Village. Lower-priced option with lovely pool area close to beach. Excellent dive base.

Kiwengwa/Pwani Mchangani
Shooting Star Lodge, tel: 077 741 4166, shootingstarlodge@ gmail.com www.shootingstar

lodge.com Refreshingly small, friendly place among cliff-top gardens overlooking sea. Pool, good food.

Pongwe
Pongwe Beach Hotel, tel: 078 433 6181, info@pongwe.com www.pongwe.com Situated on one of Zanzibar's best beaches. 16 beach and garden cottages, infinity pool.

Michamvi
Michamvi Sunset Bay, tel: 077 213 8579, simone@michamvi.com www.michamvi.com Situated by one of the best beaches in Zanzibar. Restaurant, various water sports. South African management.
Kono Kono Beach Villas, tel: 077 667 3976, reservations@konokonozanzibar.com www.konokonozanzibar.com Eleven villas with gardens and private plunge pool, on beautiful beach. 40% of resort's large plot is in plant-wildlife conservation area.

Bwejuu
Anna of Zanzibar, tel: 077 399 9387, info@annaofzanzibar.com www.annaofzanzibar.com Small, homely lodge, South African/German owned. Known for good food and service. Swimming pool.

Jambiani
Kikadini Villas, tel: 077 770 7888, reservations@kikadini.com www.kikadini.com Relatively up-market, set around central area; beautiful pool area nearby.

Blue Oyster, tel: 024 224 0163, blueoysterhotel@gmx.de www.zanzibar.de Family-run (German) hotel among palms by fine beach. No swimming pool but good value for money.
Coral Rock Hotel, tel: 077 603 1955, coraltrees@yahoo.uk www.coralrockhotelzanzibar.com Unpretentious, lively little lodge, run by group of young South Africans. Friendly atmosphere.

Kizimkazi
The Residence, tel: 024 555 5000, info-zanzibar@theresidence.com www.theresidence.com Large up-market resort by expansive tidal beach. 66 guest villas in different price categories, each with private pool. Larger pool in public central area. Spa and gym.

Pemba
Manta Resort, tel: 077 671 8852, sales@mantaresort.com www.mantaresort.com Situated in one of Zanzibar's most remote, idyllic locations, near Nzegi Forest.
Kervan Saray, resort@kayakpemba.com www.kervansaraybeach.com Unpretentious, reasonably priced 'adventurer's lodge' on secluded beach, northwest tip of Pemba, near superb dive sites, close to the endemic-rich Nzegi Forest. Swimming pool.
Fundu Lagoon, tel: 077 743 8668, reservations@fundulagoon.com www.fundu

lagoon.com Exclusive lodge by some of the Indian Ocean's best dive sites.
Pemba Misali Sunset Beach, tel: 024 223 3882, info@pembamisalibeach.com www.pembamisalibeach.com Twenty luxury seafront villas and restaurant on Chake Chake Bay.

Mafia Island
(All listed lodges/camps lower end of mid-range.)
Kinasi Lodge, tel: 077 742 4588, stay@mafiaisland.com www.kinasilodge.com British-owned, very good conventional-type lodge.
Chole Mjini Lodge, tel: 076 920 4159, www.afrikaafrikasafaris.com Less conventional, more 'outdoor-type' lodge than Kinasi but ideal for easy-going, adventurous guests.

WHERE TO EAT
Many visitors eat in their hotels, though Nungwi has a cluster of independent restaurants. In Stone Town the restaurant at **Emerson's Spice Hotel** is probably the best. Restaurants at **Serena** and **Maru Maru** hotels also notable. Simpler alternatives include **Lazuli**, **Archipelago**, and **Forodhani Open-air Food Market** (evenings).

USEFUL CONTACTS
Zanzibar Medical/Diagnostic Centre, tel: 024 223 3113, 24-hour emergency tel: 0777 750 040 or 413 714.
Good **website** for hotel/resort reviews: www.tanzaniaodyssey.com

Travel Tips

Tourist Information

Tanzania Tourist Board,
tel: +255 (0)22 211 1244/5,
www.tanzaniatouristboard.com
Arusha Travel Agency, tel:
+255 755 989 175, travel@
arushatravelagency.com
www.arushatravelagency.com
Zanzibar Tourist Corporation,
tel: +255 (0)24 223 8630,
ztc@zanzinet.com www.
zanzibartouristcorporation.net
There are many other web-
sites devoted to Tanzania and
its tourist attractions.

Entry Requirements

Passport valid for at least a
further 6 months plus entry
visa. Visas obtainable at
Tanzania's main airports and
border crossings but advis-
able to get one beforehand
through your local Tanzanian
Embassy (contact them also
for latest information).

Customs

Personal effects may be imported for the duration of your
visit duty free. A customs bond
may in infrequent instances be
demanded of visitors bringing
in expensive filming equipment
etc but most tourists will not be
troubled. Firearms require a
special permit.

A duty-free allowance is
effected on one litre of liquor,
200 cigarettes, 50 cigars or
250g of tobacco, and 250ml
of perfume.

Health Requirements

Yellow fever certificate
required if coming via country
where yellow fever present.
Visitors should seek medical
advice on anti-malarial med-
ication and on other potential
tropical diseases well in
advance of their trip. Most
visitors do not experience
serious problems.

Getting There

By Air: Many international
airlines now fly directly into
Dar es Salaam airport and
some to Kilimanjaro and
Zanzibar Airports.
By Road: Frequent luxury buses
operate between Nairobi
(Kenya), Arusha, Moshi and
Dar es Salaam. Buses also
operate between Mombasa
(Kenya), Moshi and Tanga. It is
also possible to enter Tanzania
from Zambia or Malawi. Best
companies include **Dar Express**
but dangerous driving is not
always limited to less affluent
companies.
By Rail: Not advised unless
you don't mind discomfort and
delays. First-class travel is less
arduous though far from idyllic
and you still have to use the
often abysmal toilet facilities.

What to Pack

Casual, lightweight clothing is
best in the bush. Neutral
colours are popular though not
essential. Long sleeves and
trousers help prevent mosquito
bites (but do not rely on this!),
and hats, sunglasses and comfortable shoes make life easier
and healthier when walking or
camping. In the rains light
waterproofs are handy.
Heavier clothing (sweaters/
jackets etc.) is needed in highland areas (including the
Serengeti and other higher-
plateau parks in the dry season
– mid-May to mid-October).
Ngorongoro can be particularly
cold at this time. Those climbing Kilimanjaro or Meru will
need several layers of warm
inner clothing and suitable
wind/waterproof outer clothing. Boots are also recom-

mended for more extreme altitudes. Evening or city clothes tend to be casual or smart/casual throughout Tanzania. A **camera** with at least one telephoto lens (minimum 200mm, preferably 3/500mm). Almost everyone uses digital cameras so bring spare memory cards and at least one spare battery with appropriate charging equipment; good **binoculars** (7 or 8 X 50 is adequate); if you intend to go walking or camping, you might find a small **rucksack** with a torch, penknife and portable water bottle or flask very handy.

Money Matters

Currency: Tanzania has a decimal system based on the Tanzanian shilling (TShs). Notes are in denominations of 500,1000, 2000, 5000 and 10,000 TShs.

Exchange: Foreign banknotes (especially US dollars) and travellers' cheques may be exchanged at bureaux de change or the larger hotels. It pays to shop around. There is an increasing number of banks, bank branches and ATMs in the larger towns and cities and access to your money is usually more straightforward than it once was. Avoid any temptation to change money 'on the street' as apart from being illegal it is subject to various scams.

Banks: Main banks are: Standard Chartered, Barclays, Exim, CRDB, Stanbic Eurafrican and the Bank of Tanzania. Banking hours are: 08:30 to approx. 12:30 and 13:00–16:00 Mon–Fri; 08:30–11:30 Sat; 09:00–11:30 Sun; hours vary from bank to bank.

Credit cards: Major credit cards are often accepted in the larger hotels, lodges, resorts etc., but it is best not to depend too much on them.

Tipping: Tipping for good service (about 10%) is always appreciated except when reasonable service charges are included in the bill (and when you feel confident that the service charge will be passed on to the staff).

Accommodation

Hotels are graded by a star system (often self-awarded) but also by the rather free use of words such as 'luxury', 'exclusive', etc. Hotels, beach resorts safari camps, etc. are increasing rapidly and many are expensive, so flip through the list of possibilities and reviews on the internet when planning and shop around, as a small guide like this one can only recommend a small sample of what is available.

Transport

Road: Ongoing upgrading of roads is gradually transforming the Tanzanian system. The major tourist routes now have good tarmac or gravel surfaces though secondary and minor roads can still be badly potholed and/or corrugated. Situations can change quickly and independent travellers should seek local information before departing.

Petrol and diesel are readily available along the major tourist routes and in the towns though independent travellers

to the more remote regions, including certain game parks, must be self-sufficient in terms of fuel. In the event of **breakdowns** on the open road, set up two reflective warning triangles (these are required by law) at appropriate distances either side of the vehicle. If you cannot fix the vehicle yourself, wave down a passing traveller. With locals, discuss payment before accepting help or a tow. There are **garages** in all the large towns. Not all the *fundis* (mechanics) are thoroughly trained so if possible stay with your vehicle until repairs are complete and make sure you agree on an estimated price

USEFUL PHRASES

ENGLISH	SWAHILI
Hello	*Jambo*
How are you?	*Habari?*
Fine/OK	*Mzuri*
Thank you	*Asante*
(very much)	(*sana*)
Welcome!	*Karibu!*
	(pl. *Karibuni*)
Excuse me	*Samahani*
Goodbye	*Kwaheri*
Yes	*Ndiyo*
No	*Hapana*
Today	*Leo*
Tomorrow	*Kesho*
Hot	*Moto*
Cold	*Baridi*
Hotel	*Hoteli*
Room	*Chumba*
Bed	*Kitanda*
Shop	*Duka*
One	*Moja*
Two	*Mbili*
Three	*Tatu*
Four	*Ine*
Five	*Tano*

before repairs begin. If you intend driving to remote parts of a particular game park, take a guide or notify the rangers at the park gate and/or the manager of your lodge or camp. **Car hire** is expensive compared with the USA or Europe, but there are an increasing number of car hire firms in major towns. Visitors may drive in Tanzania using a valid international driving licence, which should be carried at all times when driving. Driving is on the left. The speed limit on open roads is 80kph (50mph), except where indicated, and in towns 50kph (30mph). There are frequent police checks on major roads, sometimes with radar. Remain patient and polite if stopped, however frustrating. **Bus:** Travelling on Tanzania's crowded local buses (dalla-dallas) is not advised. The best of the long-distance buses (such as Dar Express), are reasonably comfortable and air conditioned, though they too can sometimes be recklessly driven. Routes covered include Dar/Moshi, Dar/Iringa/Mbeya, Tanga/Moshi and Moshi/

Arusha. Bus services to Nairobi and Mombasa are also available. Departure times of the main services are usually published in the local press. **Train:** There are three major railway lines in Tanzania: Dar/Tanga/Moshi, Dar/ Mwanza/Kigoma/ Mpanda and Dar/Mbeya/Zambia. Rail travel in Tanzania can be long, uncomfortable and tiring. The 'Uhuru' railway between Dar and Zambia is the most reliable and comfortable of Tanzania's railways, but first-class travel is advised. **Ferry:** Several ferry companies, among them Azam Marine, Flying Horse and Sea Star, operate between Dar and Zanzibar, from the customs jetty opposite St Joseph's Cathedral on the main Dar seafront. On Lake Victoria services run between Mwanza and Bukoba (in Tanzania), and Port Bell (in Uganda). The historical steamer *M.V. Liemba* still operates out of Kigoma on Lake Tanganyika, serving Zambia and Burundi. **NB** Most ferries are reasonably safe but there have been two major

accidents in recent years. **Air:** Air Tanzania, the national airline, is currently unreliable. Most tourists flying within Tanzania use one of several private airlines (such as Coastal, Precision and Zanair) offering scheduled flights to all major tourist destinations, as well as charter flights.

Travelling with a Local Safari Company

According to an online assessment the top three 'de luxe' safari companies are currently 'Access 2 Tanzania', 'Africa Dream Safaris' and 'Thomson Safaris', the top three 'mid-range' companies 'Across Tanzania Expeditions', 'Another Land' and 'Flash Safaris', and the top three 'budget' companies 'Duma Explorer', 'Fay Safaris' and 'Good Earth Tours'. There are, however, many more companies with excellent or very good reputations, including 'Leopard Tours', 'Roy Safaris' and (alphabetically): 'Abercrombie and Kent', 'Bobby Tours', 'Bushbuck', 'Chimpanzee Safaris', 'Dorobo Safaris', 'Flycatcher Safaris', 'Ker and Downey Safaris', 'Sunny Safaris', 'Takim's Holiday Tours and Safaris' and 'Wildersun'. Before finalizing a deal, independent travellers should confirm the main points of the agreement with the company, preferably in writing. Points should include the maximum number of people per vehicle, your exact itinerary and exactly what the agreement covers (such as game park fees, provision of back-up

	CONVERSION CHART	
FROM	**TO**	**MULTIPLY BY**
Millimetres	Inches	0.0394
Metres	Yards	1.0936
Metres	Feet	3.281
Kilometres	Miles	0.6214
Square kilometres	Square miles	0.386
Hectares	Acres	2.471
Litres	Pints	1.760
Kilograms	Pounds	2.205
Tonnes	Tons	0.984
To convert Celsius to Fahrenheit: x 9 ÷ 5 + 32		

vehicle in event of major breakdown, etc.).

Business Hours

Generally shops open by 09:00 or 10:00 and close at 17:00 or 18:00, often with a long lunchtime break (12:30 to 14:00 or 15:00). Super-markets (and small *dukas* selling groceries and general goods) often open earlier and stay open into the evenings, without a lunch break.

Time Difference

Tanzania has only one time zone, 3 hours ahead of GMT.

Communications

The Tanzanian landline tele-phone system made big improvements some years ago, with direct dialing wide-spread, but now faces serious competition from mobile phone companies such as 'Vodacom', 'Mobitel' and 'Celtel', which are hugely popular nationwide. Internet facilities exist in all cities and major towns, with wi-fi avail-able in certain places, including many of the better hotels and lodges.

Electricity

The power system is 220/230 volts AC. US appliances require an adaptor. Plugs are usually 13-amp square pin. Power cuts are fairly com-mon, though most standard tourist hotels and lodges have their own generator.

Weights and Measures

Tanzania operates the metric system.

Health Precautions

Malaria is endemic in all lowland areas below 800m (2600ft) and particularly virulent. Visitors should take prophylactics as prescribed by their doctor. A course of these should begin at least one week before entering the country, and carry on throughout and for two weeks after the stay. In the unlikely event of visitors experiencing fever on return-ing home they must seek treatment immediately and inform their doctor of the pos-sibity of malaria etc. Measures which can be taken to prevent malaria also include the use of mosquito nets at night, spray-ing of rooms with insecticide, the application of insect repellant and the wearing of long-sleeved shirts, long trousers, socks and so on in the evenings and early mornings.

Other insect-borne diseases such as **yellow fever** and **sleeping sickness** are present, but visitors should be in-oculated against the former and hardly any visitors are affected by the latter. Tsetse flies, one species of which carries sleeping sickness, can give travellers in the bush a sharp little bite, but few vic-tims suffer anything worse.

Bilharzia is a debilitating water-borne disease, caused by a parasitical worm and contracted by swimming in certain stretches of fresh water. Lake Victoria is heavily infested. It is easily avoided, by resisting any temptation to swim or wash in such waters.

AIDS is widespread in Tanzania.

Tanzania, especially during and just after the rains, has its share of **creepy crawlies**. Few are threatening, but common sense should be employed. Scorpion, snake and spider bites are very rare and seldom fatal. On the coast, spiny sea urchins and stone-fish can cause problems. The latter are rarely encountered by tourists and the threat from them and sea urchins can be lessened by wearing strong, thick-soled canvas shoes when walking through shallow sea water.

Try to avoid untreated drinking **water**, ice cubes and raw vegetables, and peel all fruit. Tap water is unsafe for drinking or brushing teeth. Mineral water is available in many local shops and restaurants, and all the better hotels and lodges will usually provide complimentary bottles in your rooms. Independent travellers should carry mineral water with them or boil or sterilize drinking water and milk.

Cuts, **bites** and **stings** are liable to turn septic if left untreated, so an appropriate ointment should be applied as soon as possible. Cuts and grazes from coral can be particularly easily infected.

Health Services
There are qualified doctors on hand in the major towns, as well as pharmacies selling a wide range of medicines. In the more popular parks many lodges and camps have qualified doctors on hand or on radio call, and in the unlikely event of major accidents or serious illness, patients would be flown out, usually quickly, to an appropriate hospital. Similarly, walkers and climbers on Kilimanjaro can expect fairly efficient medical evacuation in the event of an emergency.

Most travel companies insist on their clients taking out **medical insurance**, but if this is not the case, travellers should make sure that they insure their health before their trip begins.

Security
Petty thieving, muggings, etc. occur in Tanzania, as elsewhere. Care should always be taken of personal property.

Don't advertise your relative wealth and be careful, even when in a vehicle, of wearing jewellery as such items as watches and necklaces are sometimes snatched through open windows. Similarly, beware of pickpockets, and con-men who 'recognize' you from the airport. In the unlikely event of more serious robberies, do not resist. Drug-related problems are on the increase and it is unwise to walk around towns at night or in any lonely places by day.

Emergencies
Dial 111, 112, 999 (fire, ambulance, police).

Etiquette
It is bad mannered to wear revealing clothes especially in Zanzibar or on the coast, except when swimming etc. Shorts, of course, are acceptable in the bush and in most towns with small Muslim populations, especially in tourist areas. When shopping, dealing with taxi drivers etc., haggling is expected, except in supermarkets etc. where of course the prices are fixed. It is considered rude to take photographs of people without asking permission or (having gained permission) agreeing on a fee. Photographing Muslim women without permission is considered to be particularly offensive. In no circumstances should photographs be taken of army barracks, trucks police stations, bridges or any other sensitive buildings or areas.

Language
The national language is Swahili, though English is widely spoken in most tourist areas (*see* page 123).

GOOD READING

Brodie, FM, *The Devil Drives* (Eland)
Dugard, Martin, *Into Africa* (Bantam)
Hemingway, Ernest, *Snows of Kilimanjaro* (Random House)
Jeal, Tim, *Stanley* (Faber)
Matthiessen, Peter, *Tree Where Man was Born* (Harvill)
Mercer, Graham, *Bagamoyo, Town of Palms* (available in Dar and Bagamoyo or from gmercer@istafrica.com)
Reader, John, *Africa* (Penguin)
Stanley, HM, *How I Found Livingstone* (White Star Publications.
Stewart, Alexander, *Kilimanjaro, A Complete Trekker's Guide* (Cicerone)

Field guides:
Estes, R *Behaviour Guide to African Mammals* (Russel Friedman).
Estes, R *The Safari Companion* (Russel Friedman).
Kingdon, Jonathan, *Kingdon Pocket Guide to African Mammals* (Russell Friedman)
Richmond, MD *Guide to the Seashores of Eastern Africa* (Sida).
Richmond, MD, *Fieldguide to the Seashores of East Africa* (Dar University)
Roberts *Birds of Southern Africa* (John Voëlcker Bird Book Fund).
Zimmerman/Turner/Pearson *Birds of Kenya and Northern Tanzania* (Helm Field Guides).

INDEX

INDEX